IS-42: Social Media in Emergency Management

By FEMA

10/31/2013

Course Summary

Table of Contents:

Summary for Lesson 1

Social Media in Emergency Management

Social media has grown, not only as another major channel for broadcasting emergency communication to the public, but also as a means of conversing and engaging with the public as a whole community during emergencies.

Whether in preparation for, in response to, or recovery from an emergency event, conversations are occurring on social media networks.

Course Goal

This course provides a collection of better practices to build capabilities in the use of social media technologies in emergency management organizations and to assist them in furthering their emergency response mission.

Screen Features

- Click the **Exit** button to close this window and access the menu listing all lessons of this course. You can select any of the lessons from this menu by simply clicking on the lesson title.
- Click the **Glossary** button to look up key definitions and acronyms.
- Click the **Help** button to review guidance and troubleshooting advice about navigating through the course.
- Track your progress by looking at the **Progress** bar at the top right of each screen. To see a numeric display, roll your mouse over the Progress bar area.
- Follow the bolded green instructions that appear on each screen in order to proceed to the next screen or to complete a Knowledge Review or Activity.
- Click the **Back** or the **Next** buttons at the top and bottom of screens to move backward or forward in the lesson. **Note**: If the **Next** button is **dimmed**, you must complete an activity before you can proceed in the lesson.

Navigating Using Your Keyboard

Below are instructions for navigating through the course using your keyboard.

- Use the **Tab** key to move forward through each screen's navigation buttons and hyperlinks, or **Shift** + **Tab** to move backwards. A box surrounds the button that is currently selected.
- Press **Enter** to select a navigation button or hyperlink.
- Use the arrow keys to select answers for multiple-choice review questions or self-assessment checklists. Then tab to the **Submit** button and press **Enter** to complete a Knowledge Review or Self-Assessment.
- **Warning:** Repeatedly pressing **Tab** beyond the number of selections on the screen may cause the keyboard to lock up. Use Ctrl + **Tab** to deselect an

element or reset to the beginning of a screen's navigation links (most often needed for screens with animations or media).

- JAWS assistive technology users can press the **Ctrl** key to quiet the screen reader while the course audio plays.

Receiving Credit

To receive credit for this course, you must:

Complete all of the lessons. Each lesson will take between 10 and 20 minutes to complete. It is important to allow enough time to complete the course in its entirety.

Check the length of the lesson on the overview screen.
Remember . . . YOU MUST COMPLETE THE ENTIRE COURSE TO RECEIVE CREDIT. If you have to leave the course, do not exit from the course or close your browser. If you exit from the course, you will need to start that lesson over again.

Pass the final exam. The last screen provides instructions for how to complete the final exam.

Course Structure

This course is divided into 5 major lessons.

To help you keep track of your place within the course, the **current lesson title** is displayed in the upper left corner of each screen. In addition, a **lesson list** is presented at the beginning and end of each lesson.

The **lesson overview** states the approximate length of the lesson.
The **progress bar** is displayed in the upper right corner of each content screen to help you gauge your movement through the course.

Overall Course Objectives:

- Explain why social media is important for emergency management.
- Describe the major functions and features of common social media sites currently used in emergency management.
- Describe the opportunities and challenges of using social media applications during the five phases of emergency management.
- Describe better practices for using social media applications during the five phases of emergency management.
- Describe the process for building social media capabilities and to sustain the use of social media in emergency management organizations (state, local, tribal, territorial).

Lesson Review

This lesson provided you with an overview of the course and instructions on how to navigate through the course and how to obtain credit for taking the course.

- Review the course goal and key learning objectives.
- Review the major modules.
- Review course navigation and course credit information.

Summary for Lesson 2

Introduction

This lesson presents the case for using social media in emergency management. It emphasizes important differences between social media and traditional approaches to managing information before, during, and after emergency situations.

Objectives: At the completion of this lesson, you should be able to:

- Explain why using social media is important to emergency management.
- Identify the changes in media and public information.
- Explain the communication opportunities available to emergency managers through social media.
- Describe several examples of using social media in a variety of emergency management functions in different types of disasters.
- Identify the challenges of using social media and explore ways that these might be addressed.

Social Media is Another Communications Channel

Image: Sedalia Missouri, May 25, 2011. A car drives down the highway exploring the damage on the road and on the countryside.
[Voice of CB radio operator] "OK I've got a lot of damage out here on South 65 Highway."

[Voice of narrator reads text on the screen] Just three days after the massive tornado that struck Joplin, Missouri, an EF2 tornado struck the 20,000 residents of Sedalia, Missouri. The town suffered no casualties and survivors reported only minor injuries. Officials are quick to point out that the use of Social Media - before, during and after the storm - as one of the main reasons for the lack of injuries.

Image: Joann Martin speaks in her office at the Pettis County Health Center. She talks with members of her staff. Staff members look at FACEBOOK. Image of the DisasterAssistance.gov website is displayed on a Smartphone.

[Voice of: Joann Martin, Administrator, Pettis County Health Center] "My first alerts came through Dave's alerts and then the Sheriff's Department alerts I was able to stay in phone communication with the staff and Dave alerted everyone here that there was going to be a need for sheltering. There's a population in our community that gets their information from FACEBOOK, from texts, from non-traditional sort of communications."

Image: View of the Sedalia-Pettis County, Missouri FACEBOOK website.
[Voice of Dave Clippert, Emergency Management Director Sedalia-Pettis County, Missouri] "This is our County Emergency Management page we use to put out all kinds of different information but during severe weather we put severe weather notifications and warnings and we attempt to put pictures with that, so that people can actually see where the storm is located. We don't want to have people worried about getting hit or beat up with the storm in Northern Pettis County when the storm is only going to affect the Southern Pettis County."

Information is a Commodity

"In an emergency, you must treat information as a commodity as important as the more traditional and tangible commodities like food, water, and shelter." Jane Holl Lute, Deputy Secretary, Homeland Security (Lesperance, et. al, 2010:3)

Changes in Media and Public Information

Image: Black and White picture of family gathered around the TV
[Narrator] Old media was predominantly one way communication born from radio and TV, the model of broadcast mass media.

Image: Picture of a press release
[Narrator] The press release was the main medium for emergency managers to release critical information.

Image: Reporter at a storm site
[Narrator] The target audience for media was passive and the news cycle was much slower paced allowing for careful coding of the outgoing message to the media, public, and coordinating and cooperating agencies.

Image: Press conference with National Guard
[Narrator] Strongly based on command and control models, it worked well in controlling message content and timing as long as the news cycle maintained a consistent pace.

Image: CNN Headline News logo video image
[Narrator] With the advent of the Internet and world wide web, the news media moved to a 24-hour cycle and access to media at the site of a disaster event became more accessible and immediate.

Image: LAPD website
[Narrator] Now social media sites allow average citizens to post text, pictures, video, and links that disperse content quickly and widely.

Image: Harris County Twitter feed about fires
[Narrator] This new medium has outstripped the pace and volume of not only the standard press release but also that of the mainstream and local media as well.

Web 1.0

As the Internet matured and content evolved on the World Wide Web, not only did the volume of information expand greatly, but so too did expectations of this content.

At one time, it was simply important to get information on the web. Keeping that information current then became a challenge. Today, users and content generators expect to interact with one another directly, often in real-time.

In this way, the Internet has evolved from a static path of sharing information to a dynamic communication conduit for all to contribute.

Web 2.0

Social media differs from early Internet content in the following ways:

- Media-rich audio, video and animations are now common.
- New Internet tools permit users to create synthetic experiences that do not exist in the real world.
- These tools allow people to collaborate easily online, often at little or no cost.

Social Media Ecosystem

Screen shows icons of FACEBOOK, YouTube and Twitter.
[Narrator] The social media ecosystem is varied and includes sites that offer the following major social media functions.

Screen shows the LAFD website.
[Narrator] Blogging or "web logs" are a single- or multiple-author websites that allow for sharing a combination of text, video, and/or pictures.

Screen shows Idisaster 2.0 website page.
[Narrator] Common blogging sites and software include Blogger, Wordpress, and Typepad, although many other web tools offer this functionality as well. Most blogging sites allow readers to respond to material by posting comments.

Screen shows LinkedIn webpage for International Association of Emergency Managers.
[Narrator] In line with the popularity and widespread acceptance of text or SMS messages shared through mobile devices, microblogging has also gained in popularity.

Screen shows Twitter search for SMEM.
[Narrator] The most commonly used microblogging application is Twitter.

Screen shows KYEM FACEBOOK site.
[Narrator] Peer-to-peer sharing of longer, perpetual posts is the most common function associated with social media.

Screen shows AzEIN FACEBOOK site.
[Narrator] Sites such as FACEBOOK, Google+ and MySpace provide a platform for sharing content with friends and followers.

Screen shows LinkedIn webpage for National Emergency Management Association.
[Narrator] Special-purpose peer-to-peer networks such as LinkedIn, Xing and Plaxo, focus on delivering these same capabilities to people based on professional affiliations or other common interests.

Screen shows Flickr site for Pala Fore 2011.
[Narrator] Media sharing sites such as Flickr, YouTube, Vimeo, Tumblr and Pinterest allow users to share pictures and video.

Screen shows West Orange Emergency response team Google+ website.
[Narrator] These sites are often used in combination with blogs, microblogs, and peer-to-peer sharing sites such as FACEBOOK and Google+.

Screen shows Wikipedia website.
[Narrator] Related to peer-to-peer sharing are Wikis, the best known of which is Wikipedia.

Screen shows FEMA Wikipedia website.
[Narrator] Wikis provide a common-platform for generating and sharing articles about specific topics or subjects with input from multiple authors and editors.

Screen shows Alabama FACEBOOK website.
[Narrator] Now, we'll cover some of the more common social media sites used by emergency managers in more depth.

Blogs

Blogger, **Wordpress**, and similar platforms allow for a single author or a group of authors using one account to post content and links as a series of articles or posts arranged in a chronological sequence like a diary or journal.

Blogging sites allow users to access more content than microblogging or peer-to-peer sharing sites that also allow readers to respond by posting comments. It should be noted, that the comment feature of most blogging platforms permit users to exert varying levels of control over what appears in response to their content.

Individuals or organizations usually create blogs to chronicle their work, create a portfolio, inform others, share ideas and solicit feedback.

Twitter

Twitter is a microblogging site. It provides users with a platform for short text messages that may include web links, pictures, audio, and video content.

- The term micro is used as **Twitter** restricts users to posting short messages or "**Tweets**," as they are called, that consist of no more than 140 characters.
- **Tweets** are similar to text messaging (**SMS** or **Short Message Service**), except that they are shared publicly to anyone with access to the **Twitter** service.
- Even so, **Twitter** users typically orient their activity toward the interests of a specific audience or group of followers.
- Users can subscribe to other users' **Tweets**, send direct messages, or reply publicly.
- Users often share comments about related subjects through the use of **hashtags**. A common hashtag for social media in emergency management is **#SMEM**.

What is special about **Tweets** or **Twitter** posts is that when the account holder enables the location feature, the geodata it contains can help provide a more accurate common operating picture. This is true particularly when the posts include a picture or video.

Peer to Peer Sharing - Common Social Networking Sites

FACEBOOK, Google+, and LinkedIn are examples of social networking sites.
FACEBOOK, Google+, and LinkedIn are all social networking sites. Each of these sites allows individuals, companies, organizations, and associations to post text, video, pictures, links to other web content, or combinations of all of these electronic media.

The posted media comprise a profile.
This posted media, with some permanent and some constantly changing sections, comprises the profile of an individual or organization. Increasingly more information about the individual can be shared, such as location-based information and media preferences (music, pictures, video, etc.).

Social networking sites are different than blogs.
What differentiates these social networking sites from a blog or static web page is that they allow users to directly connect with one another, through groups or networks or even by location, when this feature is enabled. They also allow users to comment directly or to obtain a direct feed of content to their own page or mobile device for easy viewing and response.

FACEBOOK and Google+ are more widely used by the public.
FACEBOOK and Google+ are used more widely by organizations and the public to keep others up to date on their status and activities or to advertise events.

LinkedIn is focused on professionals, associations, or groups with a common interest.
LinkedIn is used more often by professionals, associations, or groups. It is a good platform to form communities of practice, for continual learning, and sharing of better practices. However, all these sites, and others like them, allow groups with a common interest to share media through a common platform.

Media Sharing Sites

Sites such as **Flickr**, **Picasa**, **YouTube**, **Vimeo**, and **Tumblr** offer hosting for pictures and videos.

Users can include text commentary, group photos or video. Editing can be performed directly on the site, including embedding certain graphics, links, or metadata such as the GPS coordinates, date and time an image was recorded in their content files.

This media can then be embedded in a blog, **FACEBOOK** page, or linked in a **Tweet**.

Wikis

Wikis are repositories for information or documents; the most well known is **Wikipedia.** Online encyclopedias typically offer subject specific areas where information can be obtained.

Another wiki example is **challenge.gov**. The Federal Government and the public put forward challenges; anyone can compete by submitting ideas, solutions, or their opinions. In particular, FEMA has posted a challenge to the public to share ideas for community-based activities to help everyone prepare for disasters.

The **Emergency 2.0 Wiki** based in Australia is another example. It's focused on creating a wiki to provide best practice advice on how to use social media and Web 2.0 in all phases of emergency management.

Content Ownership

Image: Twitter page and Main website page for Louisiana Office of Emergency Preparedness
[Narrator] It's important to remember, as noted before, that content from one social media site can be embedded or linked to content in another site.

Image: Main website page for Louisiana Office of Emergency Preparedness and FACEBOOK page for Louisiana's Governor's Office of Homeland Security and Emergency Preparedness
[Narrator] For instance, a "Tweet" from Twitter can reference a FACEBOOK post that includes a longer text posting including pictures and video.

Image: FACEBOOK page for Louisiana's Governor's Office of Homeland Security and Emergency Preparedness
[Narrator] A FACEBOOK page can include a feed from Twitter or embedded YouTube videos. Likewise, a YouTube site can include a reference back to a FACEBOOK page or link to another site on the web.

Image: FACEBOOK post for Louisiana's Governor's Office of Homeland Security and Emergency Preparedness
[Narrator] One last note to keep in mind. Each of these sites has different ways of managing content ownership. In some cases, they may own the rights to content you post and allow others to reuse, link to or share that content.

Image: FEMA website page with Press Release
[Narrator] Others may give the account owner sole rights to their content. The same holds true for archiving the data that is available. We will cover this issue in a little more depth in lesson 3.

Monitoring and Aggregating Sites

Increased access to content generation tools and the portability of these platforms through mobile computing, personal digital assistants and smartphones have spawned a rapid and steep increase in the volume of traffic generated on the web.

In order to monitor and filter the stream of social media, sites and tools have been created to sift and aggregate content into feeds tailored to individual user preferences.

Sites have also been created to monitor and rank user activity and content according to date, location, topic, relevance, popularity and other criteria to facilitate searching.

Monitoring and Aggregating Sites

Image: HootSuite, Tweetdeck, Monitter and Trendsmap icons
[Narrator] HootSuite, Tweetdeck, Monitter and Trendsmap are all sites that allow monitoring and managing social media sites.

Image: Trendsmap image
[Narrator] It enables searching for specific words, hashtags, and followers, often across different platforms; all in one place.

Image: Adding social media sites in HootSuite
[Narrator] HootSuite and Tweetdeck, for example, aggregate multiple social media site feeds in one spot and allow users to search and monitor by keywords.

Image: Trendsmap image
[Narrator] Monitter and Trendsmap provide tracking for Twitter feeds and allow users to search and monitor message streams by the location of the person generating content.

Image: Feed Stats dashboard in Google Feedburner
[Narrator] Google Feedburner aggregates and disseminates content from websites, blogs, audios, videos, and photos according to user-defined criteria. This site also provides a feature to monitor the number and identity of users who subscribe to your feeds.

Social Media Influence Ranking

Sites have also been created to monitor and rank user activity and content to facilitate searching according to date, location, topic, relevance, popularity and other criteria.

Sites that provide an analysis of a specific social media user include **Klout**, **Tweetlevel** and **Twitalyzer**.

Most of these sites provide a score for measuring social influence, using an algorithm to calculate the score based on an analysis of the number of followers, number of messages, and number of times those messages are then rebroadcast out to other recipients. These can all be used to identify individuals in a social network who have a greater level of influence through their followers.

Challenges

"Social media has added credibility challenges to the formerly unquestioned voice of the emergency manager." Tom Olshanski, Director of External Affairs at the U.S. Fire Administration

Social Media as New Media

Social media is different in that it changes media communication for emergency management in some key ways:

It is decentralized and non-hierarchical.
Not controlled by one or more entities. Anyone with access (any web enabled device, e.g. basic computer, phone) and minimal skills can post and view.

It is usually immediate and available globally.
What is publicly posted can be viewed immediately and by all, including those throughout the world.

Multi-channel (two or more ways), multivariate, and multimodal.
Multi-channel (two-way or more) posts can go out to a number of different services at one time. Posting on Twitter, FACEBOOK, and to a Blogpost all at once is not unusual.

Media are multivariate as the way and the volume of the content posted may differ depending on the medium. A FACEBOOK and Twitter post differ by the number of characters, the way they are displayed, and how the recipient receives them. Also, they may differ in the number of people who receive the message and the number of times it may be repeated, through "reTweets", linking, and reposts.

Multimodal media can consist of text, pictures, video or a combination thereof, and can be edited and reformulated with little control over how it might be presented.

The public obtains its news from multiple sources and contributes to the media discourse.
The public now obtains its news and information from multiple sources (TV, radio, and the Web) and chooses what, when, and how it wants it. In some ways, this can be viewed not as broadcasting, but as micro-channels.

The Information Chain has Reversed

"The 21st century information chain has totally reversed the traditional chain of command." James Graybeal, Deputy Chief of Staff for Communications and Director of Public Affairs, NORAD/USNORTHCOM (Lesperance, et. al, 2010:11)

Opportunities to Use Social Media for Emergency Managers

One way to look at the opportunity to use social media is to examine the government's role in providing value with respect to crisis and emergency management (Mark Moore, 1997). This is done by:

- **Providing service**: Providing services such as fire fighting or emergency medical, and coordinating the provision of post-disaster relief and recovery.
- **Achieving outcomes**: Achieving outcomes such as designing and developing mitigation measures; developing and executing emergency management plans; or coordinating and supporting the restoration of critical public utilities and services.
- **Stimulating participation**: Stimulating participation such as public engagement in personal, private, and public plans; encouraging private responses and volunteer efforts; and supporting public review and engagement in coordinating public and private efforts to prevent, prepare, mitigate, respond to, and recover from disasters. This is consistent with the "Whole Community" approach as it engages the public as part of the team, and looks at social media as another means for connecting with the public and focusing on meeting those needs in a mutual way.

Primary Mission for Emergency Management in Government

If the primary mission of government emergency management is providing service, achieving outcomes, and stimulating participation in emergency management efforts, then some of the key benefits that social media may provide towards this mission are:

- Saving lives through rapid communication.
- Communicating (more) effectively and directly with constituents.
- Reaching a larger group of constituents.
- Building situation awareness.
- Responding to new, incorrect or conflicting information.

- Building community resilience through prevention, mitigation, and preparedness efforts by the promotion of government participation and building mutual trust in the community.
- Fostering transparency and accountability.
- Reducing call volume (wired and cell) to call centers (non-emergency and emergency).

Practice in Action: Social Media Use in Emergency Management

We will now review several major examples of social media use, in a variety of emergency management functions, in different types of disasters.

Saving lives in fast moving disaster events with little or no warning
Image: Tennessee Emergency Management Agency Twitter site.
[Narrator] In Nashville, Tennessee, the Tennessee Emergency Management Agency (TEMA) uses social media to both broadcast emergency alert messages and to monitor and coordinate communication with partners and the public.

Image: Tennessee Emergency Management Agency Twitter site.
[Narrator] During the historic floods in May, 2010, TEMA used Twitter and FACEBOOK to alert the public throughout the State of flash floods and tornado warnings.

Image: Tennessee Emergency Management Agency FACEBOOK site.
[Narrator] This news was quickly re-broadcast by their followers on Twitter and FACEBOOK in a number of ways; re-Tweeted or reposted on other platforms, helping to quickly spread the message to a wider audience.

Communicating directly with constituents rather than through media, responding quickly and effectively to new, incorrect or conflicting information
Image: Kansas Division of Emergency Management Twitter site
[Narrator] The Kansas Division of Emergency Management monitors social media to track any new information, rebroadcast or direct messages from their trusted partners, other agencies or organizations and to correct any false rumors or misinformation.

Image: Kansas Division of Emergency Management Twitter site
[Narrator] They use aggregating sites, HootSuite and Tweetdeck, to filter and screen messages from several social media sites, and Twitter and FACEBOOK, looking for trends and correcting incorrect communication by directing responses to their current status updates.

Image: Kansas Division of Emergency Management FACEBOOK site
[Narrator] They also use these same platforms to broadcast their message, whether an official press conference, press release or posting, which often helps ensure that the media gets the correct message as they know that the public gets their news from multiple sources and will check one against another.

Building situation awareness
Image: Alabama Emergency Management Agency crowdsourced map
[Narrator] The Alabama Emergency Management Agency worked with a number of partners to create a "crowdsourced" map of disaster requests and services following the destructive tornadoes of April 2011.

Image: Alabama Emergency Management Agency crowdsourced map
[Narrator] With the sponsorship of Tuscaloosa News and Gadsden Times and volunteer support from American Red Cross, CrisisCommons, Humanity Road, GIS Corps, Standby Task Force, and University of Alabama, a site hosted by UCLA's Office of Information Technology mapped social media posts so individuals and organizations could match services and needs swiftly and appropriately.

Image: Alabama Emergency Management Agency crowdsourced map
[Narrator] A map of unmet needs indicates clusters where emergency managers may need to focus resources. Individuals and organizations can post both needs and available goods and services on the same site cutting out the middleman and reducing logistical demands on emergency managers.

Image: Alabama Emergency Management Agency crowdsourced map
[Narrator] Users can also use social media to connect with familiar sources of goods and services directly. Widespread access to this information through crowdsourced maps helps emergency managers build situation awareness while streamlining response and recovery efforts after a disaster.

Building community resilience through prevention, mitigation, and preparedness efforts by the promotion of participation in government and building mutual trust in the community.
Image: Louisiana Governor's Office of Homeland Security and Emergency Preparedness website
[Narrator] The Louisiana Governor's Office of Homeland Security and Emergency Preparedness uses social media in their efforts to build community resilience.

Image: Louisiana Governor's Office of Homeland Security and Emergency Preparedness Twitter site
[Narrator] Following Hurricane Katrina, the State of Louisiana made great strides to prevent and mitigate the impacts of future storms, floods, and other hazards. FACEBOOK, Twitter, Flickr, and YouTube were used as part of a strategy to inform and involve the public that included videos instructing people how to prepare themselves and their homes to withstand storm effects.

Image: Louisiana Governor's Office of Homeland Security and Emergency Preparedness website[Narrator] Likewise, they shared pictures of mitigation projects such as floodwall construction. Louisiana officials have also used social media to broadcast public hearings on updates to flood maps in the Greater New Orleans area.

Image: Craig Fugate
[Narrator] "Social media is an important part of the Whole Community approach because it helps to facilitate the vital two-way communication between emergency management agencies and the public, and it allows us to quickly and specifically share information with state and local governments as well as the public." (Craig Fugate, May 5, 2011 statement to the Senate Committee on Homeland Security and Governmental Affairs, Subcommittee on Disaster Recovery and Intergovernmental Affairs). Social media is a powerful tool to enable swift and efficient response and recovery efforts on a local basis.

These are just some of the major social media uses currently in practice by emergency managers. We will cover these in greater breadth and depth in lesson three.

Organizational Challenges to Social Media

There are some potential challenges in using social media and ways that these might be addressed.

Public agencies and public servants are under continuous pressure to expand or improve services, and reduce costs while achieving the same or better results, and protect equity while expanding representation and participation.

Organizational Challenges to Social Media

Here are some of the key organizational challenges to adopting the use of social media in an emergency management organization:

Leadership buy-in, organizational culture.
Fear and distrust of what is new or not familiar, questions about the reliability of information and the ability to verify what is provided by social media as well as, possibly, the fear of its misuse or abuse, making leaders look bad.

Organizational capability.
IT staff may not be familiar with enterprise deployment of social media or lack the infrastructure capacity to accommodate its use, especially high-definition or high bandwidth applications, such as images and streaming audio or video. Emergency management workforce may be unfamiliar with social media or might lack the skills required to use it effectively.

Sustainability (competition for resources, skills, time).
With emergency service organizations already working with lean resources and expected to do more with less, there is more competition for shrinking staff and their time. Emergency response staff members are already overloaded with their daily responsibilities.

Security policies and restrictions related to IT systems.
IT staff may perceive social media platforms as potential security risks. Organizational guidelines for their use and management may not have kept pace with the current state of web technology. Sensitive computer systems may be prohibited from connecting to social media sites.

Privacy of personal information.
Legal staff and public citizens' advocates may have concerns about citizens' privacy and personal information, including how sensitive data should be handled, tracked, stored, and used.

Public records retention requirements
Quote "Legal records retention requirements for archiving communications at State and Federal level can damper use of these tools. Many locales are not staffed to do this or the staff they have are not familiar with the technologies. Changes in legal requirements have been outpaced by adaptation of social media." Tom Olshanski,Director of External Affairs at the U.S. Fire Administration

Everyone does not have access to social media.
22% of adults do not have access to or use the Internet. Older, poorer, less educated, and rural populations tend to have less access.

Click this link to access **How the Public Perceives Community Information Systems**.

Opportunities for Social Media in Emergency Management

Let's look at the opportunities and challenges that social media tools and channels offer to achieve these benefits. These are mainly:

- **Speed**: Doing things quickly; eliminating the middleman, noise and filters between those who have information and those who need or can use it (note: bi- and multi-directional communication).
- **Relevance**: Doing the right thing; getting the right message to the right audience; focusing on influencers and interested followers in a position to act (such as public vs. media, partners, etc.)
- **Accuracy**: Doing things right; ensuring that information is correct, confirmed by independent sources and backed up by facts or direct observation.

"We used to worry about accuracy, now we worry about speed."
Tom Olshanski, Director of External Affairs at the U.S. Fire Administration

Public Expectations

Before looking at the better practices, the expectations of both the public and those providing emergency services to the public need to be considered.

We can evaluate social media in emergency management by the degree to which we meet citizen expectations. Social media should be seen as a way of influencing these expectations by engaging and leveraging the resources of the entire community.

Looking again at the model of government role in crisis and emergency management, social media can be used in emergency management to deliver greater benefits in terms of speed, relevancy, accuracy, and efficiency and to provide and convey integrity, satisfactory results, and dependability.

Social Media in Emergency Management: The Time is Now

"Social media is imperative to emergency management because the public uses these communication tools regularly. We must adapt to the way the public communicates by leveraging the tools that people use on a daily basis. We must use social media tools to more fully engage the public as a critical partner in our efforts."

Written Statement of Craig Fugate, Administrator, Federal Emergency Management Agency, before the Senate Committee on Homeland Security and Governmental Affairs, Subcommittee on Disaster Recovery and Intergovernmental Affairs: "Understanding the Power of Social Media as a Communication Tool in the Aftermath of Disasters: Release Date: May 5, 2011 Dirksen Office Building, Washington, D.C.

Key Better Practices to Support the Use of Social Media in Emergency Management

Following are key points that can be used to make the argument for adoption and use of social media in an emergency management organization:

- Explain the significant benefits and associated small risks of its use.
- Acknowledge that those unfamiliar with social media may find its use uncomfortable or intimidating. The introduction of the Internet, e-mail and the Web produced similar anxieties. Review how central the use of the Internet, e-mail and Web tools have become in business.
- Emphasize the downside of being excluded from the public conversation already occurring:
  - Do you want the public discussing your emergency or disaster without you?
  - Don't you want to know what the public is saying (about you)?
  - Do you know how to participate and respond?
- Show examples of other government users and their experiences.
- Suggest starting slowly, experimenting with a few tools, and adapting to ever-changing situations and technologies.

Click this link to access **Key Organizational Challenges**. The social media links are provided as a reference. FEMA does not endorse any non-Federal government websites, companies, applications, or products.

Case Studies: Adopting Social Media use in Emergency Management

These are some examples of how emergency managers approached the adoption of social media within their own organizations.

Image: State of Kansas Division of Emergency Management FACEBOOK page
[Narrator] From the outset some of the leadership at the State of Kansas Division of Emergency Management were not completely on board, but

understood the potential of social media. They allowed their public affairs department to develop social media behind the scenes and on a separate system, off their main computer networks.

Image: State of Kansas National Guard website
[Narrator] They were able to bring in more HR support through the National Guard by convincing leadership to bring in extra staff for video production to reach a larger audience. Their senior managers looked at it as a way to expand their reach.

Image: State of Kansas National Guard website
[Narrator] This, of course, is a natural fit with new media as social media platforms have become the largest platform for multi-media consumption. Their social media exposure has grown exponentially.

Image: Alabama Emergency Management Agency website
[Narrator] The Alabama Emergency Management Agency demonstrated the need and how social media works to their decision makers.

Image: Alabama Emergency Management Agency YouTube channel
[Narrator] The biggest selling-point came when it was used to great effect during emergency responses to major disasters in which social media engaged the whole community in disaster relief efforts.

Image: Arizona Emergency Information Network Twitter site
[Narrator] While the Arizona Emergency Information Network had the support of their senior managers, discovering even that the Mayor of Flagstaff was Tweeting to her constituents, they still took baby steps - initially, getting to know people in the social media community, figuring out who the most helpful connectors were, engaging them in conversation on social media and figuring out a way to work with them.

Image: Tennessee Emergency Management Agency website
[Narrator] The Tennessee Emergency Management Agency encountered some headwinds at first, but now has more of the wind at their backs garnering greater support for social media use.

Image: Tennessee Disaster Agency website
[Narrator] One major selling-point has been the dramatic reduction in call volumes to call centers. After seeing a huge rise in visitors to their website and FACEBOOK page and followers in Twitter, TEMA saw calls to their emergency call center drop by one-half reducing the staff hours needed to operate their call center and lifting some of the burden from the PIO.

All of these agencies agree that it is important to realize that these conversations in social media are going to take place whether you are a part of it or not. We will cover these steps and approaches in greater detail in lesson 3.

Lesson Review

This lesson presented the case for using social media in emergency management:

- Explained why the use of social media is important for emergency management.
- Reviewed the most common social media sites, their major functions, and features currently used in emergency management.
- Identified the opportunities and challenges of using social media applications in emergency management.
- Reviewed some better practices for using social media applications in emergency management.

- Introduced the process for building the capabilities to sustain the use of social media in an emergency management organization.

Click this link to access a list of **Commonly Used Social Media Sites, Platforms, and Tools by Emergency Managers**. The social media links are provided as a reference. FEMA does not endorse any non-Federal government websites, companies, applications, or products.

Summary for Lesson 3

Better Practices in Social Media Use for Emergency Management

This lesson presents better practices in the use of social media for emergency management and illustrates how emergency managers in the field have adopted social media.

Objectives: At the end of this lesson, you should be able to:

- Identify the levels an organization typically transitions through to get to a level of proficiency in use (basic, intermediate, advanced).
- Describe key and current examples of better practices in social media for emergency management.
- Identify and address how organizations have adopted and integrated the use of social media in emergency management while overcoming common challenges.

Better Practices in Social Media

Image: Photo of home at night
[Narrator] It is early morning in a suburban neighborhood. There is sound of a fire heard off in the distance.

Image: Cell phone text message
[Narrator] 5:00 AM Four Mile Canyon, Colorado

Image: Fire raging, cell phone text message, phone on desk
[Narrator] In this home, a cell phone rings with a Twitter message: There is a fire raging close to a neighbor's home. Then the home phone rings with a REVERSE 911® call to evacuate.

Image: Fire in forest
[Narrator] The mother in the family opens the window and encounters the smell of thick smoke.

Image: Red Cross Go bag, cars evacuating on the highway
[Narrator] Quickly she and her husband gather the family, grab the go bag, and pack them in the car.

Image: Cars evacuating on the highway
[Narrator] The family pulls away.

Image: Cell phone text message
[Narrator] While her husband is driving, the wife texts that they have evacuated and that they are alright. She then posts their status to FACEBOOK and Twitter, as well.

Better Practices in Social Media Use for Emergency Management

"In these really big disasters, the initial response is generally not government. It's individuals helping each other, trying to find out what's going on. … we kind of have this barrier, because the public isn't official. It's not an official source of information... But we've seen now in the U.S., from wildfires in California and Boulder to the recent ice storm and snowstorms...the public is putting out better situation awareness than many of our own agencies can with our official datasets."

Craig Fugate, Administrator of the Federal Emergency Management Agency
Haiti: the Importance of Social Media Use During a Disaster, Jan 19th, 2011

Developing Social Media Use in Emergency Management

Before we move into the better practices, it will be helpful to look at the ways in which organizations typically develop social media use in their emergency management organizations.

Let's begin by revisiting the model for the role of government during a crisis, presented in Lesson 2:

Providing service

Providing service such as fire fighting, emergency medical services, and coordinating the provision of post-disaster relief and recovery.

Achieving outcomes

Achieving outcomes such as designing and developing mitigation measures; developing and executing emergency management plans; and coordinating or supporting the restoration of critical public utilities and services.

Stimulating participation

Stimulating participation such as public engagement in personal, private, and public plans; encouraging private responses and volunteer efforts; and supporting public review and engagement in coordinating public and private efforts to prevent, prepare, mitigate, respond to, and recover from disasters. This is consistent with the "Whole Community" approach, which engages the public as part of the team; looks at social media as another means to connect with the public; and focuses on the mutual meeting of needs.

Developing Social Media Use in Emergency Management

- Providing service
- Achieving outcomes
- Stimulating participation

We can look at social media as a means (one of many) by which emergency managers can provide **service** to the public, achieving a successful mutual **outcome** of protecting the public and mitigating the impact of disasters. The **participation** in social media is the bridge between the means and the end when the emergency management community and the public work together.

We will build on this concept with the following model.

Matrix of Social Media use in Emergency Management

The following matrix provides a useful model for understanding the levels of social media practice and where the various uses relate to that matrix.

While these are not necessarily discrete stages, each of these can be considered levels of more strategic and sophisticated use that engages more closely with the pubic.

Level 1 - Monitor

In the monitoring stage, emergency managers watch and listen to messages streaming through social media to better understand the medium and the message. Taking time to become familiar with the talk and the tempo of social media helps emergency managers establish what military commanders often call their battle rhythm.

Monitoring focuses on one-way communication *from the public*. This mode informs and instructs the Emergency Manager before any action is taken to deploy or use social media tactically or strategically.

This approach allows emergency managers to focus on the means by which the public gathers, shares and responds to information about emergencies. It does not necessarily involve the delivery of a service to secure a particular outcome. Nevertheless, effective social media monitoring can inform response decisions and influence plans for its strategic use.

Level 2 - Command/Control

Level 2 involves one-way communication to the public intended to inform, convince, compel, or instruct. This approach emphasizes the use of social media as a tactical means of achieving strategic objectives by motivating public action. It is intended to deliver a service - timely public information - that is communicated directly to the public. It neither assumes nor requires direct public participation. However, many emergency managers find it helpful to engage social media savvy volunteers to augment scarce staff resources when employing this approach.

Level 3 - Coordinate

Level 3 starts a conversation; the emergency manager engages in 1- or 2-way communication with others to avoid or minimize resource and information conflicts. The use of social media at this stage is ends focused.

At this level, emergency managers engage the public through social media to both gather and disseminate information. This starts a one-to-many/many-to-one conversation that helps the public update the situation awareness of emergency managers and other users, while obtaining information from them that guides a more efficient and effective response to the emergency. When the public and emergency managers have a shared understanding of the situation and what's at stake, they can take independent action without fear of compromising the outcome.

Level 4 - Cooperate

This stage involves more direct engagement between individuals or groups and emergency managers. This two-way communication facilitates shared understanding of the situation, which shapes participants' expectations of the means of responding or the ends to be achieved. The result is shared resources, allowing participants to achieve multiple objectives. Crowdsourced maps are a prime example of social media use at this level.

Level 5 - Collaborate

At this stage, participants' communication and engagement creates a shared understanding of the situation. It produces a common commitment to pursue the same results by working together. This level of engagement is characterized by in-depth dialogue and shared effort among participants. The use of wikis and shared document portals to produce emergency plans or recovery documents are examples of efforts at this level.

Better Practices in Social Media Use for Emergency Management

We will now present key and current examples of better practices in social media for emergency management.

Note: Although there is no guarantee, these social media practices can deliver the following benefits.

Saving Lives Through Rapid Communication

Social media is used for alerting the public in sudden onset and rapidly developing disaster situations. In disasters such as tornados, earthquakes, wildfires, flash floods, and shooting incidents, microblogging sites such as **Twitter** and **FACEBOOK** are used to quickly deliver messages warning the public of hazards.

Saving Lives Through Rapid Communication

Image of the Navajo Nation Department of Emergency Management website.

[Narrator] Social media is used for alerting the public in sudden onset and rapidly developing disaster situations such as the use of Twitter by the **Navajo Nation Department of Emergency Management**. The Navajo Nation occupies a vast area of 27,000 square miles in northeastern Arizona, the southeastern portion of Utah, and Northwestern New Mexico. Many of its tribal members live in remote areas. The Navajo Nation Twitter account **@navajonation** is used to post community news. This news feed has also been used for emergency alerts in a number of disaster events.

Image of the Navajo Nation Twitter account displaying a Tweet about the earthquake that hit the area.

[Narrator] On July 13, 2009, the tribe posted links to information on an earthquake that hit the area including hashtags related to the event, **#navajoearthquake** and **#Navajo,** and linking to the US Geological Survey and local news media.

Image of the Navajo Nation Twitter account displaying a Tweet about the Flagstaff fires.

[Narrator] In June 2010, the Navajo Nation Tweeted updates on the Flagstaff Fire. These Tweets helped keep tribal members on the periphery of the fire informed. Using hashtags helped communicate with those who may not follow their Twitter account and increased the visibility of both incidents to other users. Emergency management staff of the Navajo Nation monitor Twitter feeds to track, respond, send and reTweet information of interest to their community.

Infographic illustrating the earthquake and twitter comments. Courtesy of http://www.leadgenix.com.

[Narrator] The speed of social media is well illustrated by messages sent during the magnitude 5.8 earthquake that struck Northern Virginia in August 2011. The temblor was felt as far away as New York City, where Tweets about the event arrived many seconds before anyone felt the first shake.

Saving Lives Through Rapid Communication

Image of the Guam Homeland FACEBOOK page.

[Narrator] Within minutes of the news breaking about the devastating earthquake that struck off the coast of Japan in March 2011, in Guam both cellular and landline communication lines were disrupted. Computer servers were overloaded, and radio reception was hampered.

Image of the Guam Homeland FACEBOOK post about the earthquake.

[Narrator] Due to the groundwork in social media use laid by the Guam Homeland Security Office of Civil Defense, they were able to use sites such as **FACEBOOK** and **Twitter** to help communicate the possibility of an impending tsunami. They dedicated a person full-time to **FACEBOOK** to monitor and communicate throughout the event and used it to address questions from the public.

Image of the Guam Homeland FACEBOOK post about the earthquake.
[Narrator] In addition, they posted their message to every broadcast stations' **FACEBOOK** page and found that the public was actively posting their 'post' to their page to help spread updates on the tsunami. By tagging the Office of Civil Defense to their post, it made the information more credible.

Communicating (more) Effectively and Directly with Constituents

Social media sites can be used to communicate directly with constituents rather than through the media. In some ways, this helps to keep the media in line with your direct message because the public has access to both your feed and that of the commercial media.

Communicating (more) Effectively and Directly with Constituents

Image of the California Department of Forestry and Fire Protection website and the Great Fire Flickr website.
[Narrator] The **California Department of Forestry and Fire Protection**, known as **Cal Fire**, has an extensive social media presence and utilizes a combination of YouTube videos and feeds direct from the field utilizing **Skype** (a popular voice-over-internet-protocol) to provide on the spot news of wildfires to the public.

Image of the California Department of Forestry and Fire Protection Twitter website.
[Narrator] They also use **Twitter** to provide alerts on wildfires and use their **FACEBOOK** page to inform the public on preparedness and prevention programs, as well as, fire condition updates.

Image of the California Department of Forestry and Fire Protection FACEBOOK website.
[Narrator] Using **Twitter** and **FACEBOOK** for alerts is very similar to REVERSE 9-1-1® technology and the **Emergency Alert System (EAS)**. As explained earlier, social media can be considered another set of communication channels to those who rely predominately on the Internet for their information.

Reaching a Larger Group of Constituents

In a far different way, social media can help fill the gap in communication during a disaster when wired communications or electricity fails. Smartphones and other web-enabled wireless devices often allow access to information when other services fail.

Cellular networks and Internet services that rely on fault-tolerant fiber-optic networks also fill gaps in regions with scattered population where news media or community notification services may be unable to get the word out efficiently.

Reaching a Larger Group of Constituents

Image of earthquake damage.
[Narrator] In January 2010, a 7.0 Magnitude earthquake struck Haiti, taking the lives of over 316,000 people, injuring 300,000, leaving over a million people homeless, and impacting another 3 million, making it one of the most devastating natural disasters ever.

Image of cell messages.
[Narrator] Although the communications infrastructure was virtually destroyed, individuals were still able to use their cell phones to send out (SMS) text

messages broadcasting their location, status, needs for help, road closures and other critical information.

Image of rescue works in rubble.
[Narrator] These texts were tracked, mapped, often by remote volunteers based in other countries, and used by search and rescue teams, relief workers and other aid agencies to focus the humanitarian response.

Image of earthquake damage.
[Narrator] Volunteers outside the affected area translated and organized this information so that emergency responders and citizens on the ground could focus on more immediate needs and access the information to locate those in urgent need to provide direct assistance.

Building Situation Awareness

Social media can build situation awareness, culling data to obtain a clearer operating picture.

Building Situation Awareness

Image of road closed and Twitterfall page showing information about the ice storm.
[Narrator] During the severe snow and ice storms in the Pacific Northwest at the beginning of 2012, emergency managers in Seattle, Tacoma, Vancouver, and Bellevue in Washington State, just to name a few, used social media monitoring and aggregation sites such as **Tweetdeck, HootSuite, Twitterfall, Monitter,** and **Trendsmap** to send out alerts.

Image of cars in the snowstorm and Trendsmap page showing information about the ice storm.[Narrator] They used social media to track road conditions, power outages, accidents, and other major damage and effects of the storms and to pinpoint impacts and emergency service requirements in those areas. Their well-established and broad-based social media network enhanced the level of trust the community had in their efforts making it more likely the public would share what they knew and enlist their own personal networks to extend the reach of emergency communications.

Responding Quickly and Effectively to New, Incorrect or Conflicting Information

During disaster events, rumors and misinformation can spread quickly over social networks.

While social networks are often self-correcting when it comes to misinformation, active intervention by emergency managers to dispel rumors and spread new information to the public using social networks is common practice.

Responding Quickly and Effectively to New, Incorrect or Conflicting Information

Image: City of Rocky Mount FACEBOOK page
[Narrator] Dispelling rumors and spreading new information to the public were just some of the ways that the City of Rocky Mount, North Carolina used **Twitter** and **FACEBOOK** to great effect during **Hurricane Irene**. The city government actively monitored social media and discovered several rumors.

Image of FACEBOOK page showing animals in pet shelters
[Narrator] One involved a horrible rumor that animals in the pet shelters would be euthanized prior to the hurricane.

Image of Twitter post about dam bursting
[Narrator] Another indicated the Tar River Reservoir Dam was about to burst. Emergency managers quickly dispelled these rumors through posts on **FACEBOOK** and **Twitter**.

Image of Twitter post about power outage
[Narrator] Over the same platforms, they also broadcast news about closed roads and health and safety information following a power outage.

Building Community Resilience Through Prevention, Mitigation, and Preparedness Efforts by the Promotion of Participation in Government and Building Mutual Trust in the Community

Emergency managers are using social media not only to deliver prevention and mitigation messages, but also use these platforms to engage the public in a dialogue and encourage feedback on efforts to keep the public safe and secure.

"Participating in the process of government provides other benefits. If citizens feel empowered, communities get benefits in both directions. Those who believe they can impact their community are more likely to be engaged in civic activities and are more likely to be satisfied with their cities and towns."
How the Public Perceives Community Information Systems,   Pew Internet Project and the Monitor Institute.

Click this link to access **How the Public Perceives Community Information Systems**.

Building Community Resilience Through Prevention, Mitigation, and Preparedness Efforts by the Promotion of Participation in Government and Building Mutual Trust in the Community

Image: Clark County, Washington Regional Emergency Services Agency website with 30 Days, 30 Ways campaign details
[Narrator] To celebrate **National Preparedness Month**, the Clark County, Washington Regional Emergency Services Agency's **30 Days, 30 Ways** campaign engages the public in a preparedness contest that challenges citizens to come up with one new way to prepare themselves for emergencies every day in September.

Image: Clark County, Washington Regional Emergency Services Agency FACEBOOK post
[Narrator] They used several platforms, including their blog, **FACEBOOK**, and **Twitter** sites, to engage the public to participate.

Image: Clark County, Washington Regional Emergency Services Agency FACEBOOK post
[Narrator] One of the great features of this initiative is that it allows citizens to share and engage not only with the agency, but with each other, helping to create a stronger sense of community that also helps build resilience.

Image: Finalists in contest are announced
[Narrator] Participating in the process of government provides other benefits. If citizens feel empowered, communities get benefits in both directions. Those who believe they can impact their community are more likely to be engaged in civic activities and are more likely to be satisfied with their cities and towns.

Images of FACEBOOK post about the Guam Homeland Great Shakeout program and children participating in the program
[Narrator] The Guam Homeland Security Office of Civil Defense has achieved tremendous penetration with their emergency preparedness message. For example, the "**Great Shakeout**" campaign for earthquake preparedness had over 58,000 participants out of a population of 180,000 people; 15,000 more

than the previous year, in large part due to the communication through social media sites; posting the campaign on the pages of their followers and news outlets.

Images of FACEBOOK post about earthquake preparedness
[Narrator] They send out frequent messages encouraging the public to prepare a "**Go Kit**", and also post messages from other agencies such as power outages. Using these tools, they can answer immediate questions.

Images of FACEBOOK post about run/walk
Narrator] During **National Preparedness Day,** they hosted a 5K run/walk, and **FACEBOOK** was a major tool to spread the word, creating an event and inviting all their followers on **FACEBOOK**.

Image of participants posing with a disaster preparedness kit
[Narrator] Another campaign, **Ready Guam**, asks **Twitter** and **FACEBOOK** users to simply post a picture of themselves with a disaster preparedness kit to win a T-shirt with the words **#Ready#Guam**. This simple campaign engages the public to take a proactive approach in being prepared.

Fostering Transparency and Accountability

Social media platforms and the utilization of media posting sites such as Flickr, YouTube, and Vimeo are used to demonstrate preparedness and response efforts, helping to foster greater transparency of the work done by emergency management agencies with the public.

Fostering Transparency and Accountability

Image: Operation Smoky Hill video image of firefighters in drill exercise
[Narrator] A good example of demonstrating transparency and accountability is this **YouTube** post of **Operation Smoky Hill**, conducted at Crisis City in Saline County, Kansas, a state of the art training center.

Image: Operation Smoky Hill video image of firefighters in drill exercise
[Narrator] The exercise was run by the Kansas Division of Emergency Management, a division of the Kansas Adjutant General's Department. The exercise seeks to display and evaluate emergency response to a domestic terrorism scenario.

Image: Operation Smoky Hill video image of firefighters in drill exercise
[Narrator] This exercise involved 300 first responders from local, State and Federal agencies involved in emergency response.

Image: Operation Smoky Hill video image of firefighters in drill exercise
[Narrator] These types of multimedia posts are just one of many ways the Kansas Division of Emergency Management shares information with the public.

Image: Screen shot of How the Public Perceives Community Information Systems document
[Narrator] "Those who think local government does well in sharing information are also more likely to be satisfied with other parts of civic life such as the overall quality of their community and the performance of government and other institutions, as well as the ability of the entire information environment in their community to give them the information that matters."

Crowdsourcing and Measurement of Reach and Continuous Improvement

There are some more advanced social media uses.

The first, the use of **crowdsourcing,** is aimed at building mutual trust in the community, which in turn helps build more resilient communities.

Crowdsourcing and Measurement of Reach and Continuous Improvement

Image: One person with light bulbs over his head and a crowd with light bulbs over their heads.
[Narrator] What is **crowdsourcing**? **Crowdsourcing** is outsourcing work tasks to the "crowd".

Image: Group of people working together in a conference room.
[Narrator] The crowd might be a loosely organized group of volunteers all the way to a tightly knit organization that has vetted staff and volunteers. These volunteers might be both in, around, and outside the affected disaster area, and the work might be tasks as:

Image: Tweet about the Navajo earthquake
[Narrator] Monitoring and searching social media sites for important posts during a disaster and in recovery.

Image: FACEBOOK entry about the rumor at Rock Mount Animal Shelter
[Narrator] Verifying the authenticity of the information and analyzing the post for any geodata, alerts, needs or other relevant factors.

Image: Map of East Coast with data points highlighted
[Narrator] Tagging and mapping by data points, for example: time, location, need, service.

Image: Map with data points highlighted
[Narrator] Developing and adapting software applications such as **free and open source software (FOSS)** for the needs of a particular organization or disaster event.

Crowdsourcing Communication During a Disaster

Image: **CrisisCommons** website page
[Narrator] **Crowdsourcing** data and volunteers is exemplified by the **Ushahidi** application and groups such as **CrisisCommons** (CrisisCamps) and **HumanityRoad**.

Image: Ham radio operator
[Narrator] Just like ham radio operators, who are used by emergency managers, using volunteers from **CrisisCommons** or **HumanityRoad** or other electronic community volunteers is similar.

Image: HumanityRoad website page
[Narrator] **CrisisCommons**, **HumanityRoad**, and **Standby Volunteer Task Force** are three such specialized groups that have provided volunteers to assist in these emergency crowdsourcing endeavors.

Image: QLD flood crisis map with Ushahidi example
[Narrator] One of the common software applications that is used for crisis data mapping is the **Ushahidi** platform. **Ushahidi** is a free and open source software that can be used for information collection, visualization and interactive mapping based on social media posts from a multitude of platforms, whether they are **SMS, Twitter, FACEBOOK**, or other social media sites.

Image: YouTube video screen capture of Ushahidi Haiti animation
[Narrator] During the response to the earthquake in Haiti of January 2010, Ushahidi was used by a spontaneous cadre of volunteers to map **SMS, Twitter**, and other web posts.

Image: YouTube video screen capture of Ushahidi Haiti animation
[Narrator] The effort grew so rapidly that the **Ushahidi Haiti** site became the defacto map for the incident with NGOs and government organizations using it for their response efforts: search and rescue, relief supplies, and other recovery work.

Image: Depicting Snowmageddon and Ushahidi example

[Narrator] During the snowstorms in Washington, DC, of 2010, or **Snowmageddon** as it was called, **Ushahidi** was used not only for crowdsourcing information and volunteers but also crowdfeeding of help; serving as a platform for peer-to-peer assistance; linking those in need with those who can give. This helps to create greater community resilience.

Measurement of Reach and Continuous Improvement

The second advanced practice involves measuring the impact of social media efforts over time. Data analysis tools such as **Klout**, **Tweetlevel** and **Twitalyzer** allow users to measure the relationships between various social media accounts and their followers. These tools help users understand and improve their reach and influence.

There is no single "right way" to measure impact or effectiveness of your social media program. Multiple measurements are recommended. By relying on a single measure, you're likely to miss important dimensions of your program.

Measures include:

- Number of subscribers.
- Number of people retransmitting your information.
- Third-party measures of social media "influence".
- Documented stories of people who credit your social media accounts with knowledge gained or actions taken during or after an event.

Emerging methods for measuring social media impact include doing surveys of community members or giving shelter users the chance to tell how they learned of shelter locations.

Measurement of Reach and Continuous Improvement

Image: Kansas Division of Emergency Management FACEBOOK website
Image: Kansas Division of Emergency Management logo and number of "likes" on FACEBOOK
Image: Kansas Division of Emergency Management Twitter header

[Narrator] The **Kansas Division of Emergency Management** uses these analytic tools to help their public information team determine whether their strategy benefits the public and which they consider the ultimate measure of success for emergency management.

Image: Kansas Division of Emergency Management Klout rating

[Narrator] The team assesses these benefits directly and indirectly by asking the following questions:

Image: Kansas Division of Emergency Management TweetLevel rating

[Narrator] **Popularity**: How many followers do we have?

Image: Kansas Division of Emergency Management TweetLevel weighted scores

[Narrator] **Influence**: Are posts and Tweets "liked", commented on, or reTweeted?

Image: Kansas Division of Emergency Management TweetLevel followers score

[Narrator] **Engagement**: Do our followers engage our material by responding to posts, sharing them, or including and tagging them in their own posts?

Image: Kansas Division of Emergency Management TweetLevel summary

[Narrator] **Trust**: Do followers consider the information we post credible?

Image: Kansas Division of Emergency Management Klout rating
[Narrator] The measurements generated by these analytic tools help them to evaluate what parts of their strategy are working and what steps they might take to improve their performance. They can also use these measures to look at ways to adjust their content and grow their network.

Adopting and Integrating the Use of Social Media in Emergency Management

"Don't look at the glitz, the glamour, and the flashiness of the newness of the technology as 'that's an end state'. It is merely another way that we need to continue to empower the public to have greater ownership and understand the roles and responsibilities they have and to provide them the knowledge, so they can make the best possible decision for them and their families in a time of crisis... and to help each other, their neighbors, while we focus on the things we do best which is helping to make a community safe, rescue the injured and trapped, and begin the process of getting the community moving towards recovery."

Craig Fugate, Administrator Federal Emergency Management Agency, From Social Data and Emergency Communications Aug. 12, 2010 American Red Cross WDC

Adopting and Integrating the Use of Social Media in Emergency Management

- We will identify and address how other organizations have adopted and integrated the use of social media in their emergency management.
- We will focus on how organizations have overcome the challenges.

As stated before, the process of development and expansion is not linear. Many agencies find that their use of social media accelerates during a disaster.

Common Steps to Adopting the Use of Social Media in Emergency Management

Focus first on the outcome you wish to achieve.
Establish the outcome that you wish to achieve: With whom are you communicating and why? What is the content of the communication? What is the intent of the message or what do you need to know?

Be prepared to adapt how you engage your audience.
Be prepared to adapt how you engage your audience through social media as you and your audience explore applications and their limitations. Create an emphasis on making your tools and communication accessible through mobile means.

Choose a few tools and develop them well.
Many new users to social media start with one platform, become comfortable with the communication and its relationship to existing operations, and then slowly start to use other social media platforms, naturally picking them up, learning, and expanding. This evolution includes integration between social media platforms and organizational websites, and the use of multimedia sites that provide a natural progression with links to multi-media.

Create a trial account before creating an official one.
While still operating out in the open, creating a trial account allows you to gain familiarity before rolling out your official presence. This will give you the opportunity to make some mistakes, operating under the radar, without having them publicized broadly at the start.

Establish a support structure.
Develop a support structure, including human resources, who will manage the accounts within guidelines, creating policies and procedures when necessary, and

train others at all levels in their use. Be creative in using current staff and cross train staff on the different platforms used.

Use subject matter experts to help with data collection.
Social media management and measurement can be complicated; using subject matter experts who understand the field can help utilize the wealth of data available.

Develop a mentorship and demonstrations from experienced users.
Wading into the language of social media may be like reading a foreign language. It can help to have those who are familiar with the platforms explain the terms and usage so all staff can communicate effectively. Pairing staff that understand the platforms with those who are less familiar is a good way to bridge the knowledge gap.

Establish news feeds (RSS).
Establishing a news feed or using RSS (Really Simple Syndication) allows an organization to publish new content on a website, blog, or other news, and syndicate this to subscribers. The feed is a summarized text of the original web page along with metadata, such as date, ownership, title, and description. News feeds make it easier for people to subscribe to your web pages without having to go and visit.

Leverage partners and volunteers.
Partner agencies and volunteers, whether independent or under the umbrella of an organization, should considered. Establish connections, both formal and informal, where you can coordinate your messages or activities before, during, and after an emergency. This helps everyone involved to communicate with one voice. Use trained volunteers, either collocated or remote, to help increase your capacity to manage social media communication, in particular during a crisis when social networks are lit up with posts.

Make people available to answer questions.
Remember that social media is a conversation, not just a broadcasting channel. Make sure you have staff who can monitor your social media sites on a steady basis, using an aggregating tool or other regular update, and reply to questions or correct misinformation when they appear.

Trust the public, the community's most wired citizens.
Encourage participation and public feedback to encourage ongoing investments in social media use. Social media communities are surprisingly self-correcting when users are out of line or feed incorrect information, although they do require some level of involvement by an organization. However, engaging with the public and allowing them to actively communicate with your organization can bring about a greater relationship of mutual trust.

Click this link to access **Common Steps**.

Develop a Strategy

Another route, although much slower, is to develop a strategy, including:

- Form a social media committee to support its use.
- Set goals: identify the audience and explain the benefits that will be derived from social media use and how risks will be mitigated.
- Develop simple metrics for evaluating the benefits, some qualitative and some quantitative.
- Define an "online persona" or "character" for your online presence; this may or may not be the same as your offline presence.
- Establish practical and transparent reporting and analysis processes, and track progress to measure program success.
- Set expectations and include some room for mistakes.

- Ensure legal language is included where needed. Make sure that promises are kept.
- Integrate social media into the organization's business: website, operations, exercises, and plans. Continuously improve on its use in after-action reviews and improvement plans.

Strategic Integration

As emergency managers and their agencies become more actively engaged with their communities using social media, they usually find it necessary to modify their approach to using traditional media. Social media has already affected the way journalists do their jobs; many of them are already well positioned to interact with emergency managers through social media rather than through conventional press releases.

Public information officers (PIOs) usually find social media helps them stay current with the continuous news cycle.
Because the operational tempo increases quickly in emergencies and disasters, **Joint Information Systems** need to address the use of social media in disseminating information and monitoring the message in the media before an event unfolds. Whether we like it or not, the disaster-affected public and many responders already have a social media presence.

Successful communication depends upon PIOs and incident commanders establishing and aligning communication priorities to incident objectives early, and updating them often during the response phase. Defining hashtag conventions and key messages for each hazard will help PIOs and others hit the ground running when disaster strikes.

Strategic Integration

Example: Many Twitter users localize their hashtags by starting with the two-letter state abbreviation or the three-letter city airport code, followed by a hazard-specific abbreviation, e.g.: wx for weather; eq for earthquake; fire for fires; police or pd for police; traffic for motor vehicle crashes.

Expert Tip: The **Tweak-the-Tweet** protocol developed by Kate Starbird, a PhD student at the University of Colorado, Boulder, provides a more complete elaboration of protocols for formatting emergency messages on Twitter for easy searching and indexing.

Final Notes on the Approach to Adopting Social Media for Emergency Management

The following are some final notes on the approach to adopting social media for emergency management:

Open vs. closed approach to social media use: Organizations choosing to implement social media strategies have a choice between approaches that can be characterized broadly as open or closed.

Some important questions to consider concerning an approach to social media:

- Does any organization really have command and control immediately following a disaster?
- Can any organization control communication in a social media environment?
- What is gained or lost by restricting, sharing, or ceding that control to the public?

Open Approach

Open policies prescribe the overarching objectives or destination of a social media strategy. They encourage experimentation and exploitation of opportunities consistent with these objectives by all employees.

Advantages: Open policies present the greatest opportunity to achieve the kind of engagement that builds trusted relationships with communities. With fewer controls, the open approach can be implemented much faster, be more flexible with changes, and more responsive to the public's expectations.

Disadvantage: May result in some early mistakes, making some managers uncomfortable with less command and control over official communication.

Closed Approach

These policies restrict the use of social media to designated personnel using specific platforms or services in a prescribed fashion.

Advantages: Complies with traditional command and control systems, ensures consistency of official communication.

Disadvantages: Takes much longer to implement. May be less flexible and responsive to the public's expectations.

Final Notes, Continued

It is important to get leadership buy-in. Defining what leadership can do to support the use of social media will help allay fear that use of this new medium will be viewed with hostility or suspicion. As mentioned before, the following are some key steps that might be taken:

- Explain the benefits of its use and the small risks associated with it.
- Acknowledge that there may be a fear of what they do not understand or have a familiarity with. This fear is similar to that of the introduction of the Internet and Web. Explain how the Internet and Web have become widely adopted and integrated to a point where e-mail, web pages, text (SMS), etc., are simply a means of doing business.
- Highlight the possible downsides of not being included in the conversation.
  - Do you want the public discussing your emergency or disaster without you?
  - Don't you want to know what they are saying (about you)?
  - Do you know how to participate and respond?
- Show examples of other government users and their experiences.
- Suggest starting slowly, experimenting with a few tools, and be ready to adapt to ever-changing situations and technologies.

Click this link to access **Key Organizational Challenges**.

Lesson Review

This lesson presented better practices in the use of social media for emergency management and how social media has been adopted by emergency managers in the field including:

- Identifying the levels that an organization typically transitions through to get to a level of proficiency in use (basic, intermediate, advanced).
- Describing key and current examples of better practices in social media for emergency management.
- Identifying how other organizations have adopted and integrated the use of social media in their emergency management and overcome the challenges.

Summary for Lesson 4

Using Social Media: Practice using Scenarios

Objectives: At the completion of this lesson, you should be able to:

- Demonstrate how some of the better practices in social media in emergency management would be used in a simulated event.
- Identify where you or your organization are on the development scale (levels) and what actions you might take.

Scenario

In the following exercise, you will have the opportunity to demonstrate your knowledge of some of the better practices in social media use in emergency management.

You will be guided through a small-scale simulation and presented a number of scenarios using a fictional county office of emergency management.

At critical points you will be prompted for appropriate answers. Make your decisions and provide answers based on which social media tools and approaches you might use to address the question or issue posed.

While we know that social media is not the sole means to address the issues in each of these scenarios, we want you to consider how social media would be used as part of or as the primary means to address them.

Considering the Possibilities

You are the Director of the Office of Emergency Management (OEM) in Liberty County, Columbia State USA.

Liberty County has been hit hard in the past couple of years by severe weather disasters that have impacted a number of your communities: historic floods, wildfires, and a major tornado.

If that was not enough, recent budget cuts had led to some staff reductions in your OEM, and you have increasingly found a need to turn to community-based organizations, volunteers, and other municipal and county workers to bolster your response efforts. These efforts have helped each community rise to the occasion in their respective responses to and recoveries from these disasters.

Considering the Possibilities

While senior government officials at the State and County levels have been satisfied with the response based on traditional media reports, there have been some concerns raised and even a few criticisms leveled at your office's communication and coordination of the response. Several civic leaders have received feedback from County citizens that they did not know what was going on or what to do during some of the disasters. Some specific feedback you received was:

- Some people with disabilities were not able to easily find assistive services.
- Several segments of the county struggled with language issues for non-native English speakers.
- Geographically isolated communities with little access to mainstream media felt that they were out of the communication loop.

You have heard about the use of social media at the State level and from other colleagues and have started exploring its use.

Background information on Liberty County:

- Population: 300,000
- Households: 122,000
- Housing Units: 146,000
- Median Age: 36
- Average household size: 2.6

Building on Accomplishments

You have gotten off to a good start. You have added accounts on **Flickr** and **YouTube** allowing you to showcase your exercises and preparedness activities in the community.

The Commissioner is very pleased and reports that the Board of Supervisors has commented very positively about the social media presence, and that the public sees the county government in a new light.

Handling Situations and Requests

What actions might you take with your social media approach to address some of the issues raised?

Some community groups would like to repost your content.

Allow them to repost; follow this and see where you can support them; increase your reach. Ensure your content is represented properly.

One group has posted some incorrect information about services provided by your County OEM.

Correct the information by adding a comment and post. Link to correct information. Post on all social media accounts. Monitor any additional communication on this.

You notice that the association of nursing homes in your county has a FACEBOOK page and active Twitter account. Getting them involved in emergency preparation has been challenging for you in the past.

- Monitor their accounts, follow the conversation, and take part in the conversation where appropriate.
- "Follow" their Tweets and FACEBOOK page.
- Direct Tweet or post as a comment when information directly relevant to them comes available.

One of your junior staff members has been posting some non-public organizational information on his personal Twitter account.

- Speak with the staff member and explain why her/his actions are not acceptable.
- If there is a written policy, explain the policy.
- If there is not a policy, consider putting one in place.

Maintaining the Conversation

You have made some progress and have 10,000 **FACEBOOK** and 1,500 **Twitter** followers.

1,200 people have viewed various **YouTube** videos and hundreds have viewed your **Flickr** photos.

The local Rotary featured your social media presence in one of their meetings, and a major news channel regularly reposts your **Twitter** and **FACEBOOK** postings.

Maintaining the Conversation

How do you address these issues using social media?

Some of the community leaders along the riverfront towns have expressed their concern over a lack of awareness of flood mitigation measures that business, home, and building owners might undertake.

Engage community groups through their social media presence (if available). Begin a conversation around plans for mitigation in concert with the towns and their leaders. Consider a survey and/or other means for outreach where social media can play a component (although not the sole component).

One day your call center receives a large number of calls regarding a concern over pandemic flu.

- Verify flu concerns by checking with public health officials.
- Once the information has been verified, update the call center and your social media sites.
- Monitor social media traffic about the flu, correct or inform as appropriate.

Taking it to the Next Level

After a number of major emergency responses over the year or so since you started using social media, your organization has a well-established social media presence with **FACEBOOK**, **YouTube**, **Flickr** and **Twitter** accounts with a large group of followers.

Your organization actively monitors and collaborates with several social networks, some managed by community-based organizations. The Commissioner of Public Safety has mentioned the more cutting-edge uses by some other counties in Columbia; you have been asked for a strategy on how to increase your reach and effectiveness through social media.

Where are You on the Matrix?

With what you have learned so far, identify where you and your organization are on the development scale and what actions might be taken.

Where is your organization on this development scale? Click on the link below. **Note:** this is not necessarily linear; do your best to determine where your use may be in specific emergency management phases.

Click this link to access **The Typical Stages of Development in the Use of Social Media**.

Next Steps

Where do you want to take yourself and, your organization, and what steps do you plan to take? *Please write these down.*

Tools and Resources to Support Developments

You may encounter challenges along the way in gaining acceptance and implementing your plan.

What resources or tools might help in the adoption of these practices? *Please write these down.*

Click this link to access **Key Organizational Challenges**.

Your Action Plan

Develop an action plan(s) for implementing social media or advancing its use in your work or organization.

This plan should include:

- Support for maintaining these practices, such as joining a social networking group.
- Periodic public forums.
- Creating an assessment of social media use, etc.

Please write these down.

Lesson Review

This lesson helped demonstrate how some of the better practices in social media in emergency management would be used in a simulated event including:

- Identifying where you or your organization is on the development scale (levels).
- Determining what actions you might take.

Summary for Lesson 5

Course Review and Listing of Additional Social Media Resources for Emergency Managers

Objectives: At the completion of this lesson, you should be able to:

- Discuss the major points from the course.
- Identify resources for continual learning about social media in emergency management.

The Business Case for Social Media Use in Emergency Management

Image: CNN video image of Japanese Earthquake
[Narrator] On March 11, 2011, a devastating 9.0 Earthquake struck 80 miles east of Sendai, Honshu, Japan.

Image: CNN video image of tsunami hitting Japanese coast
[Narrator] The earthquake unleashed a tsunami that flooded up to five miles inland, laying waste many coastal communities, killing more than 30,000 people and rendering hundreds of thousands homeless.

Image of woman using cell phone
[Narrator] Japan is a nation steeped in high technology with mobile phone penetration among the highest in the world and widespread social media use.

Image of Social Media map in Japan
[Narrator] Social media sites became a major conduit for communication about the disaster's impacts, requests for assistance, and information on access to services and help. Countless survivors shared what they witnessed through their own personal posts, pictures and videos.

Image of Twitter feed for Red Cross assistance
[Narrator] Japan and the world community, aided in part by such detailed information, responded with both moral and material support.

Image of FACEBOOK site posting survivor information
[Narrator] What's more, the Japanese people, as they have done before in hard times, banded together, now using social media sites to gather and share information, using the means of crowdsourcing information and crisis mapping to create increased situation awareness.

Image of Global Disaster Relief FACEBOOK website
[Narrator] As we have seen earlier in this course, this example of social media use demonstrates the capacity for the public and emergency managers to positively influence each other by exchanging information.

Image of Help Japan Now Red Cross QR Code
[Narrator] The relationships formed by using social media can build resilience in the face of disaster, helping a community and society as a whole meet these challenges and come through stronger.

The Business Case for Social Media Use in Emergency Management

Social media provides the capability of the public to influence the decisions and actions of government (and vice versa), leading to a greater commitment to mutual objectives.

These relationships play key roles in transforming emergency management policy and creating a culture committed to resilience.

Current Better Practices in Social Media Use for Emergency Management

The following is a summary of the current better practices in social media for emergency management covered in this course:

- Saving lives through rapid communication.
- Communicating (more) effectively and directly with constituents.
- Reaching a larger group of constituents.
- Building situational awareness.
- Responding quickly and effectively to new, incorrect or conflicting information.
- Building community resilience through prevention, mitigation, and preparedness efforts by the promotion of participation in government and building mutual trust in the community.
- Fostering transparency and accountability.
- Crowdsourcing communication during a disaster.
- Measuring reach and continuously improving.

It is important to note that as social media changes on a regular basis, with new platforms, sites, apps, and other new functions and features, practices in emergency management will evolve with them. That is why it is important to stay current with the public's use of social media and with fellow emergency management practitioners and subject matter experts. At the end of this course, a list of additional resources is provided for that purpose.

Click this link to access **Better Practices**.

Adopting the Use of Social Media in Emergency Management

We identified the major steps to adopt the use of and manage the challenges to social media in an emergency management organization.

Common Steps to Adopting the Use of Social Media in Emergency Management

- Focus first on the outcome you wish to achieve
- Be prepared to adapt how you engage your audience
- Choose a few tools and develop them well
- Create a trial account before creating an official one
- Establish a support structure to help with data collection
- Develop a mentorship and demonstrations from experienced users
- Establish news feeds (RSS)
- Leverage partners and volunteers

- Make people available to answer questions
- Trust the public, the community's most wired citizens

Click this link to access **Common Steps**.

The Typical Stages of Development in the Use of Social Media

Level 1 Monitor	Level 2 Command	Level 3 Coordinate	Level 4 Cooperate	Level 5 Collaborate
Listening in order to get your battle rhythm	Broadcasting	Conversation	Discussion and Analysis	Synthesis and Value Creation
One-way communication *from the public*, intended to inform and instruct (the EM).	One-way communication *to the public*, intended to convince, compel, instruct.	One or two-way communication, intended to avoid or minimize conflict.	Two-way communication, intended to facilitate shared expectations.	Two-way communication that produces shared meaning and objectives.
Means focused	Means focused	Ends focused	Shared means and ends	Shared means and ends
		Prevention Preparation Mitigation Response Recovery		

Continuous Learning About Social Media in Emergency Management

Social media practices in emergency management are constantly evolving.

Here are additional resources for social media in emergency management and reference information for them:

Click this link to access **Social Media Sites**. The social media links are provided as a reference. FEMA does not endorse any non-Federal government websites, companies, applications, or products.

Click this link to access a list of **Commonly Used Social Media Sites, Platforms, and Tools by Emergency Managers**.

While this course is focused on strategic better practices in the use of social media for emergency management, here is a list of **tactical better practices**. This document is not meant to be an exhaustive list of these practices, as the nature of social media is constantly changing and evolving.

Click this link to access a **List of Tactical Better Practices**.

Lesson Review

This lesson presented a summary of the courses including:

- Reviewing the major points from the course.
- Identifying resources for continual learning about social media in emergency management.

List of Commonly Used Social Media Sites, Platforms, and Tools by Emergency Managers

Note: while other sites and platforms may be used for the purposes given below. The list below represents those most commonly used by emergency managers in the USA. The list is not meant as a comprehensive presentation of all social media sites, or an endorsement of any of these sites or platforms.

Blog Sites: allow for a single author or a group of authors using one account to post content and links as a series of articles or posts arranged in a chronological sequence like a diary or journal.

Site Name	URL	Free/Cost	Main Features	Important Notes
Blogger	http://blogger.com	Free	All sites offer similar features including posting text, pictures, video, and links to other sites, and integrated with other social media sites. Posts are typically archived and can be searched, saved, edited, and deleted.	Software may be used with a custom domain but is not free and open source software (FOSS)
	http://blogspot.com	Free		
Wordpress	http://wordpress.org/	Free		Wordpress is FOSS but must be hosted. Has more features available than Blogger.
	http://wordpress.com	Blog can be hosted by Wordpress for free or paid.		Must pay to use a custom URL and to remove ads from your site (ads will be permitted if used for free)

Microblogging: a micro-blogging site provides users with a platform for short, text messages, that may include web links, attached pictures and links to video.

Twitter	www.twitter.com	Free	Message are limited to 140 characters, similar to text messaging (SMS or Short Message Service) except that it is typically shared with a group of people and most often are public. Users can subscribe to another user's Tweets, send direct Tweets or connect to them, and share a common thread through the use of what are called hashtags.	Unless the user decides to restrict their Tweets from being searched. They are all public and can be searched, aggregated, and analyzed. Tweets or Twitter posts, when the location feature is enabled by the account holder, contain geo data that, when linked to pictures or video, can help provide a more accurate common operating picture.

Course Title: Social Media in Emergency Management

Course#: IS-042

Peer to Peer Sharing- Common Social Networking Sites: these sites allow individuals, companies, organizations, and associations to post text, video, pictures, links to other web content and combinations of all of these electronic media. This posted media, some sections permanent, other sections constantly changing, comprise the profile for an individual or organization. Increasingly more information about the individual can be shared such as location based information, media preferences: music, pictures, video, etc. that they allow users to connect with one another directly, through groups or networks or even by location when this feature is enabled. They also allow other users to comment directly or obtain a direct feed of content to their own page or to a mobile device for easy viewing and response.

Site Name	URL	Free/Cost	Main Features	Important Notes
Facebook	www.facebook.com	Free- Facebook allows advertisements on right sidebar	Allows short blog posts, text chat, inbox, pictures, video, and integration with other social media sites. Live-streaming video and video chat.	Currently the largest global social network
Google+	plus.google.com	Free- Need to sign up with a Google account		New social network started by Google and looking to grow larger network.
LinkedIn	www.linkedin.com	Free- Premium account available with more features.	Similar features to those given above, except that the primary use is for professional and business networking, by companies, organizations, association and individuals. Used by many communities of practices (COPs) for sharing better practices.	Some groups are open while others are restricted and require invitations to join. Messages can only be sent to other users if they are within your network (by opt-in) unless a premium account is paid for.

Course Title: Social Media in Emergency Management
Course#: IS-042

Media Sharing Sites: These sites offer hosting for pictures, audio, videos, and other multi-media. Users can often include text commentary, group photos or video together, edit them directly on the site, and also embed certain graphics or links in the media. This media can then be shared through links, text message, embedded in a blog, Facebook page, or included in a Tweet.

Site Name	URL	Free/Cost	Main Features	Important Notes
Flickr	www.flickr.com	Free	Picture hosting. Can tag, group, and edit photos (through third party applications)	
Picasa	Picasa.google.com	Free	Picture hosting. Can tag, group, and edit photos.	
Vimeo	www.vimeo.com	Free	Hosting for video. Allows for management and tracking number of viewers.	Unlimited HD video upload.
YouTube	www.youtube.com	Free	Hosting for video. Allows editing, management, and tracking number of viewers.	Limited upload amount of HD video

Course Title: Social Media in Emergency Management
Course#: IS-042

Wikis: These sites are repositories for information or documents and typically offer subject specific areas where information can be shared and obtained. **Note:** just as there are many blogs hosted, there are many wiki sites available. Below is a listing of those that are known that are just a couple related to emergency management.

Wikipedia	www.wikipedia.org	Free	Offers a wide range of user generated listings in multiple languages and subjects.	The most famous the wikis, Wikipedi or the online encyclopedia, is where the name wiki was first used
FEMA Idea Scale	http://fema.ideascale.com/	Free- account required.	This community is for FEMA stakeholders to have a dialogue about emergency preparedness, disaster response and recovery, and other emergency management topics. While this is not strictly a wiki, it functions as a means of sharing information in the emergency management community of practice (COP).	Ideas can be voted and commented o by other users in the community.
Emergency 2.0 Wikis	http://emergency20wiki.org/	Free	Focused on creating a community for best practice advice on how to use social media and Web 2.0 in all phases of emergency management.	Based in Australia

Monitoring and Aggregating Sites: These sites and platforms provide functions to monitor and filter the stream of social media into feeds tailored to individual user preferences. These sites, depending on their features, allow for sorting feeds from social media sites by keywords, hashtags, and geographic coverage. **Note:** Most of these sites require an account on the aggregation platform and access to an account through which social media sites will be searched.

Site Name	URL	Free/Cost	Main Features	Important Notes
Feedburner	www.feedburner.com	Free	Google Feedburner aggregates and disseminates content from websites, blogs, audio, video, and photos according to user-defined criteria. This site also provides a feature to monitor the number and identity of users that subscribe to your feeds.	This site does not allow for monitoring social media sites on a stream.
Hootsuite	www.hootsuite.com	Free	Hootsuite allows monitoring and managing social media sites by keywords and hashtags. It also allows for disseminating information to multiple social media accounts.	A popular aggregating site for emergency managers due to its multiple column format.
Monitter	www.monitter.com	Free	Monitter provides tracking for Twitter feeds and allow users to search and monitor message streams by the location of the person generating content. It only allows disseminating posts through Twitter.	
Trendsmap	www.trendsmap.com	Free	Trendsmap provides tracking for Twitter feeds and allow users to search and monitor message streams by the location of the person generating content. It allows disseminating posts through Twitter and Facebook.	Good mapping feature, using Google maps.
Tweetdeck	www.tweetdeck.com	Free	Tweetdeck allows monitoring and managing social media sites by keywords and hashtags. It also allows for disseminating information to multiple social media accounts.	A popular aggregating site for emergency managers due to its multiple column format.
Twitterfall	www.twitterfall.com	Free	Twitterfall allows monitoring and managing social media sites by keywords, hashtags, and geolocation. It only allows disseminating posts through Twitter.	

Course Title: Social Media in Emergency Management
Course#: IS-042

Social Media Influence Ranking: sites that provide analyses of a specific social media user. Most of these sites provide a score for measuring social influence, using an algorithm for calculating the score based on an analysis of the number of followers, number of messages, and number of times those messages are then rebroadcast out to other recipients. They can all be used to identify individuals in a social network who have a greater level of influence through their followers.

Note: most of these sites require an account with one of the social media sites at which you are looking to seek a ranking for a user account.

Site Name	URL	Free/Cost	Main Features	Important Notes
Klout	www.klout.com	Free	Measures trust and influence on Facebook, Twitter, LinkedIn, Foursquare, and Google+.	Can also compare level of influence on certain topics using keywords. Easiest to understand and use. Covers a wide range of social media sites.
Tweetlevel	http://tweetlevel.edelman.com/About.aspx	Free	Measures influence according a wide range of criteria: Following, Followers, Updates, Lists, Updates over time period, Name Pointing, Retweets (quoted and edited), Replies, Broadcast to engagement ratio Idea Starter Score, Topsy Influence Score, Involvement Index, Velocity Index, Weighting	Offers complex analytics. There is a premium offering that is only available to a select group.
Twitalyzer	http://twitalyzer.com/index.asp	Free trial. Then charge per month depending on individual,	Measures a wide range of criteria: impact, engagement, influence, velocity, generosity, signal, clout, followers, followed, and	Offers complex analytics, at a cost.

Course Title: Social Media in Emergency Management
Course#: IS-042

			lists.	

Course Title: Social Media in Emergency Management
Course#: IS-042

Sites:

www.sm4em.com
http://www.emergency20wiki.org/wiki/index.php/main_Page
http://wiki.crisiscommons.org/wiki/SMEM_Initiative
https://communities.firstresponder.gov/
http://connectedcops.net/?page_id=2

Twitter:
   #SMEM
   #smemchat

LinkedIn: NEMA
http://www.linkedin.com/groups?about=&gid=2471654&trk=anet_ug_grppro

Blogs:

http://ww2.crisisblogger.com/
http://idisaster.wordpress.com/
http://www.engagingothers.com/
http://crisiscommscp.blogspot.com/
http://chiefb2.wordpress.com/
http://www.cpsrenewal.ca/
http://barryradford.wordpress.com/

Crowdsourcing Volunteer Groups:
http://crisiscommons.org/
http://www.humanityroad.org/
http://blog.standbytaskforce.com/

Course Title: Social Media in Emergency Management
Course#: IS-042

The Typical Stages of Development in the Use of Social Media

Level 1 Monitor	Level 2 Command	Level 3 Coordinate	Level 4 Cooperate	Level 5 Collaborate
(Listening in order to get your battle rhythm) One way communication *from the public*, intended to inform and instruct (the EM).	(Broadcasting) One way communication *to the public*, intended to convince, compel, instruct.	(Conversation) 1 or 2 way communication intended to avoid or minimize conflict.	(Discussion & Analysis) Two way communication intended to facilitate shared expectations.	(Synthesis and Value Creation) Two way communication that produces shared meaning and objectives.
Means focused	Means focused	Ends focused	Shared means and ends	Shared means and ends
Prevention				
Preparation				
Mitigation				
Response				
Recovery				

Course Title: Social Media in Emergency Management
Course#: IS-042

Key Organizational Challenges to Social Media in Emergency Management:
Better Practices to Address Them

Key Organizational Challenges	Better Practices to Address Challenges

Leadership Buy-in and Organizational Culture
Fear and distrust of what is new or not familiar, questions about the reliability of information, and ability to verify what is provided by social media; May be fear of its misuse or abuse making them look bad.
	• Explain the significant benefits and the small risks of its use.
	• Acknowledge that those unfamiliar with social media may find its use uncomfortable or intimidating. These anxieties are similar to those that accompanied the introduction of the Internet, email and web use. Review how central the use of the Internet, email and web tools have become in business.
	• Emphasize the downside of not being included in the public conversation already occurring;
	   o Do you want the public discussing your emergency or disaster without you?
	   o Don't you want to know what they are saying (about you)?
	   o Do you know how to participate and respond?
	• Show examples of other government users and their experiences
	• Suggest starting slowly, experimenting with a few tools, and adapting to ever-changing situations and technologies

Organizational Capability IT staff may not be familiar with enterprise deployment of social media or lack the infrastructure capacity to accommodate its use, especially high-definition or high-bandwidth applications such as images and streaming audio or video. Emergency management workforce may be unfamiliar with it or might lack the skills required to use it effectively.	• Develop a support structure, including human resources who will manage the accounts with guidelines (policies and procedures when necessary), and training in their use at all levels. • Have those who are familiar with those platforms explain the terms and ways they are used so that all staff can communicate effectively. • Pair staff who understand the platforms with those less familiar to bridge the knowledge gap.
Sustainability (competition for resources, skills, time) With emergency service organizations working with lean resources and expected to do more with less, there is more competition for shrinking staff and their time. Emergency response staff are already overloaded with their daily responsibilities and training in emergency protocols and other IT systems.	• Be creative in using current staff to enhance what you want to do and cross train staff on the different platforms used. • Identify reliable volunteer pools within the community with the requisite skills and commitment for cooperation in areas of social media use such as monitoring and coordinating communication.
Security Policies and Restrictions Related to IT Systems IT staff may perceive social media platforms as potential security risks and guidelines for allowing their use and management may not have kept pace with the current state of web technology.	• Use social media on computer systems that are off the organization's main computer network and do not link it with any internal systems. • Work with the IT staff to identify areas of concern and work together to problem solve. • Develop guidelines on social media use with IT staff.
Privacy of Personal Information Legal staff and public citizens advocates may have concerns about citizens' privacy and personal information, how it will be handled, tracked, stored, and used. **Public Records Retention Requirements** Legal records retention requirements for archiving communications at State and Federal level can damper use of these tools. Many locales are not staffed to do this or the staff they have are not familiar with the technologies. Changes in legal requirements have been outpaced by adaptation of social media.*	• Ensure legal language is included where needed. Make sure that promises are kept. • Establish practical and transparent reporting and analysis processes, and track progress to measure program success. • Make sure that you have staff who can monitor your social media sites on a steady basis using an aggregating tool or other regular update. • As above under organizational capacity, ensure that staff are cross trained on platforms and guidelines for use.

* Quote from Tom Olshanski, Director of External Affairs at the U.S. Fire Administration.

Tactical Uses of Social Media in Emergency Management[1]

The FEMA Course **Social Media in Emergency Management** largely covers better practices that are strategic in nature. This list is intended to address tactical uses of social media in emergency management. While some tactics may be used during all phases of an emergency, others may be specific to one or more phases of an emergency or particular to a kind of social media platform or social media site.

Improving the effectiveness and reach of your social media strategies requires a commitment to developing relationships in this medium with the public. We can make better use of social media by realizing that every post, every tweet, every share, every plus is an opportunity to learn what others appreciate and how it can have a positive impact on their lives. Following these set of tactical guidelines can help you make LEARNING POP!

Note: This list of social media tactical uses in emergency management is not meant to be an exhaustive list of all those in use nor is it meant as a static list, recognizing that emergency management practices associated with social media are constantly evolving. It is strongly suggested that these tactics be reviewed and evaluated for their effectiveness on an ongoing basis and as social media platforms change and new features and tools enter the market.

L -- Listen. The first and most important step in building a successful social media presence is listening.

- Learn the language of Social Media before an event. If your agency is not familiar with social media, then learn the associated jargon now, before an emergency strikes. The last thing you want to be doing during an event is trying to figure out what a retweet is or how to read a tweet[2].

    o Find out more about hashtags and Twitter use at:
      http://support.twitter.com/articles/49309-what-are-hashtags-symbols
    o Find out more about acronyms on Twitter: http://tinyurl.com/7tb2qxd

    There is a list of common Twitter hashtags in general use for emergency management, both in discussion on this topic and general preparedness, included at the end of this document.

---

[1] This list of tactical better practices in social media use for emergency management was culled from several sources referenced in this document. It is largely based on a blogpost by Mark Chubb, Interim Fire Chief, Woodinville Fire & Rescue .

[2] From http://idisaster.wordpress.com/2012/01/04/top-7-lessons-on-sm-from-la-arson-fire-event/ based on the experience of the L.A. Arson Watch Task Force

Course Title: Social Media in Emergency Management
Course#: IS-042

- Learn what interests others and how they engage one another is essential to gaining acceptance from other social media users.
  - One of the most important ways of showing your interest is in following and *friending* others online who share your interests.
  - Most social media users find few things more annoying than finding their stream filled with messages from social media dilettantes, so limit the number of messages you send and spread them out so others feel they can get a word in edge-wise.
  - Use your social media presence to gauge public sentiment and information needs, then post what the public is asking for.

- Keep track of information shared about your agency to help detect rumors and misinformation quickly and make it easier to correct misinformation before it spreads. During all phases of emergency management, but in particular during a disaster response, communication needs to be tracked[3]:
  - Track blogs via Google Blogs and Google Alerts, aggregate on Google Reader.
  - Track traditional media through Google News and aggregate on Google Reader again.
  - Identify keywords and hashtags (#) on Twitter that are relevant to the incident. Use tools such as hashtags.org, Twubs, Trendsmap, Kurrently, Social Mention and more.
  - Determine where your followers are, what's trending near you and other location-based searches through tools such as: Trendsmap, TwitterMap, or Monitter.
  - Monitor trends, hashtags and tweets with tools such as Hootsuite, Tweetdeck, Monitter, Netvibes, Tweetgrid and others.
- For verifying crowd-sourced data see the following report by Patrice Cloutier, one of the leaders in social media emergency management field: http://www.crowdsourcing.org/document/verifying-crowdsourced-social-media-reports-for-live-crisis-mapping-an-introduction-to-information-forensics/8811

E — Share Experiences. Really, nobody wants to know what you had for lunch today. But they just might find your choice of lunch-spot interesting if you have something to say about the service, quality or atmosphere where you dine. In other words, share the experience not just the event.

- Keep information short and to the point but keep it interesting. Post information that's relevant, timely and actionable; always include a link back to your agency's Website and other agency social media platforms.
- For blogs during the non-emergency phase and for preparedness, people are much more interested in how something made your feel than what you did. Give them something to relate to, and they will come back for more.

A -- Ask. Everybody has an opinion, but nobody has all the answers. Questions make us think.

- Like listening, asking questions gives others the opportunity to offer insights and experiences and shows members of your network that you value their opinions. Making social media interactions true conversations requires give and take. Questions make it clear you want feedback and do a better job of stimulating thoughtful responses than even the most provocative statements.

---

[3] This list was gathered and edited from Emergency 2.0 Wiki http://emergency20wiki.org/wiki/index.php/Monitoring#Monitoring_the_emergency

Course Title: Social Media in Emergency Management
Course#: IS-042

R -- <u>Repeat</u>. If imitation is the highest form of flattery, then repeating, sharing and extending the reach of what others have to say is a very close second. Social media demonstrates just how small and interconnected our world is. We tend to repeat and share only those things that resonate most deeply with our core beliefs and attitudes. And authentic, interesting, intimate, or moving images and messages only achieve universal appeal through widespread dissemination across the web of social networks we inhabit.

- During an emergency make sure to repeat critical information every so often as the life of a tweet is very short.
- Share critical information from partner agencies in a timely fashion. Remember that speed trumps accuracy.

N -- <u>News</u>. The reach of traditional media has become increasingly limited as each of us and those with whom we connect becomes a source of information about what's happening and what it means. We still rely on others to stay in touch with parts of our world beyond our reach, but we no longer assume that traditional sources and mainstream media have any particular advantage over ordinary people.

- Since Twitter only allows for 140 characters, this helps tailor short, simple, factual statements that can be readily approved. Forget word-smithing: stick to the facts and get the info out-the-door.
- As we learned from the earthquake in Haiti, during an emergency assume that communication will be limited. While still getting your message out on as many platforms as possible, some social media platforms may not function, so you also want to focus your communication within the constraints of those possible limitations. Take into consideration that on Twitter messages longer than 140 characters will be truncated; make sure to make Twitter messages SMS compatible by keeping them simple and to the point, including only critical information. If the message is longer than one tweet, then reference that the two or more tweets are connected.

I -- <u>Insight</u>. As noted above, hard, cold facts have their place, but people are more likely to relate to your insights if they shed light on the meaning or impact of an event as opposed to simply offering a restatement of the already available facts. This applies doubly to those instances when those facts are in or of themselves novel, neglected or otherwise surprising.

N -- <u>eNlarge</u>. Just as others' insights offer a glimpse into the meaning of small details we might otherwise overlook, we also need others to help us keep things in context or put them in the proper perspective. Despite the tendency of social media to amplify things that might otherwise seem incredibly trivial, social media does an incredibly good job of connecting us and others to a wider sense of what's valuable, important or even transcendent.

- Follow partner agencies, organizations, and the media, as well as community influencers and leaders. Often those you follow will in turn follow you. Following others can help grow your group of followers, making it easier to disseminate information quickly.

  When working in a Joint Command/multi-agency put systems in place for a social media presence before an event[4].

---

[4] From http://idisaster.wordpress.com/2012/01/04/top-7-lessons-on-sm-from-la-arson-fire-event/ based on the experience of the L.A. Arson Watch Task Force

Course Title: Social Media in Emergency Management
Course#: IS-042

- Agencies work hard to establish trust with their constituents and audiences, particularly on social media platforms, so there could be fear that joining under one name would diminish not only their presence but their ability to highlight their contribution to the response effort. These concerns can be ameliorated beforehand if they are understood and addressed. It is also important for all the agencies involved to understand the potential rewards and benefits of working under one name.
- Establish joint accounts before an event occurs. If you use these accounts each time for similar events, then public familiarity with them will rise.

G -- Gratitude. One of the ways social media achieves its mass appeal and ability to influence what we think and how we act is through its ability to facilitate reciprocity. The act of engaging others is, in and of itself, a way of saying thanks for connecting and sharing your world with me. Of course, it still doesn't hurt to say thank you from time-to-time.

Public—Trust the Public and Encourage their Tech Readiness.

- Trust that the public, who are proficient in these tools, will do the right thing most of the time. The public will answer each other's questions, often before you even have a chance to respond and will also shout down people who make really stupid or insulting comments. This can allow a government agency to simply ignore this kind of behavior. However, it is still prudent to have a take-down policy stated on your "info" tab that describes how comments will be handled if they do cross the line.
- Get the word out to the public about social media access to your communication. For non-emergency communications, encourage the public to use text messaging, e-mail, or social media instead of making voice calls on cell phones to avoid tying up voice networks. Data-based services like texts and emails are less likely to experience network congestion. They can also use social media to post status updates to let family and friends know they are okay. They can also use resources such as the American Red Cross's Safe and Well program.
- In addition to standard personal and household preparedness, an important component is tech readiness. See the following list on how the public can prepare: http://www.ready.gov/get-tech-ready

Prepare—During an emergency be prepared to staff 24/7 and have your communications strategy ready.

- When planning for a social media presence, include staffing measures for 24/7, even if that means using volunteer services or partnering with other agencies. Facebook and Twitter are a beehive of activity by the public and reporters. It is preferable to be on those platforms in order to not only provide information, but also to monitor the conversation. Make sure employees have access to social media from their desktop computer and mobile means (smartphone or mobile laptops).

Course Title: Social Media in Emergency Management
Course#: IS-042

Make sure that you have prepared messages for all hazards that require only event specific information to be added and then sent out. Developing some predefined hashtags and keywords to use for a type of hazard. For example Jeff Phillips, Emergency Management Coordinator, Los Ranchos de Albuquerque, New Mexico has established some set hashtags for emergency communication such as #NMEM, #NMFire, #NMStorm and #NMwx.

Using some of the aggregating sites referenced in the course for multiple platforms can help with this and to prime the pump so when you have to push out emergency messages to multiple platforms, you will be ready.

Twitter Hashtags Related to Social Media for Emergency Management[5]

General Hashtags

#SMEM = Social Media & Emergency Management [Used to share info on the intersection between social media & emergency management. You may see articles shared, questions posed and broad information-sharing.]

#SMEMChat = Used during Friday one-hour conversations on Twitter between 12:30p-1:30ap EST
#EM = Emergency Management
#EGov or #OGov = Electronic Government or Open Government
#Gov20 = Government 2.0 references government use of online tools, broader than

Emergency Management
#HSEM = Homeland Security Emergency Management (discussion underway about using this instead of SMEM to designate incident underway)
#SM = Social Media
#WX = Weather-Specific Tweets (for state-specific, these will be preceded by state initials).
#2BeeRdy = Grassroots Preparedness Website at http://2BeeReady.org
#CoEMS = Chronicles of EMS
Conference & Association Hashtags
#NEMA = National Association of Emergency Management
#IAEM = International Association of Emergency Management
#UASI = Urban Area Security Initiative
#VSMWG = Virtual Social Media Working Group (w/ DHS Science & Technology Directorate)
#IAEMETC = IAEM Emerging Tech Committee

In order to facilitate further discussion, FEMA created the following hashtags:

#imprepared used to encourage individuals and families to get prepared; #kidsfiresafety used to encourage parents to practice fire safety tips;
#howihelp (in partnership with the ARC)used to encourage people to talk about how they help their neighbors and communities.

---

[5] List of Hashtags courtesy of Cheryl Bledsoe, Emergency Management Division Manager at the Clark Regional Emergency Services Agency http://www.sm4em.org/active-hashtags/

How the Public Perceives Community Information Systems

Studies in three cities show that if people believe their local government shares information well, they also feel good about their town and its civic institutions. Those who are avid information consumers from news media and online sources are more likely to be involved and feel they have impact

Lee Rainie, Director, Pew Internet Project

Kristen Purcell, Associate Director-Research, Pew Internet Project

Tony Siesfeld, Director of Research, Monitor Institute

Mayur Patel, Director of Strategic Assessment and Assistant to the President, Knight Foundation

3/1/2011

http://pewinternet.org/Reports/2011/Community-Information-Systems.aspx

Pew Research Center's Internet & American Life Project
1615 L St., NW – Suite 700, Washington, D.C. 20036   202-419-4500 | pewinternet.org

How the Public Perceives Community Information Systems

When people think about issues in their communities, they usually frame those issues through practical questions they would like to see addressed. Is the town budget too high or too low? Are teachers doing a good job? Are the streets safe? Do emergency responders have the right training? How can traffic congestion be eased? Does the library have the best technology for patrons? Do zoning rules work the best way? Are all the people in the community getting fair access to social services?

The way that people address questions like those is to gather, share, and act on information. Yet there is not much knowledge about how the parts of a community's information system work and fit together. Believing it would be useful for communities to examine how well their own information systems were performing, the John S. and James L. Knight Foundation asked the Monitor Institute to explore key components of local information systems in three communities with advisory help from the Pew Research Center's Internet & American Life Project. This report is the fruit of an eight-month research effort pilot testing several research methods in Macon, Philadelphia, and San Jose to probe key parts of those systems. Some of findings, especially in surveys conducted in the communities, were notable and surprising:

- Those who think *local government does well in sharing information are also more likely to be satisfied with other parts of civic life* such as the overall quality of their community and the performance of government and other institutions, as well as the ability of the entire information environment in their community to give them the information that matters.

- *Broadband users are sometimes less satisfied than others with community life*. That raises the possibility that upgrades in a local information system might produce more critical, activist citizens.

- *Social media like Facebook and Twitter are emerging as key parts of the civic landscape and mobile connectivity is beginning to affect people's interactions with civic life*. Some 32% of the internet users across the three communities get local news from social networking site; 19% from blogs; 7% from Twitter. And 32% post updates and local news on their social networking sites.

- If citizens feel empowered, communities get benefits in both directions. *Those who believe they can impact their community are more likely to be engaged in civic activities and are more likely to be satisfied with their towns.*

These surveys were part of an exploratory period of research by the Monitor Institute and the Pew Internet Project that used several methodologies to examine the components of local information systems that were highlighted by the Knight Commission on the Information Needs of Communities in a Democracy, a joint project with the Aspen Institute. The Commission argued in October 2009 that a healthy democratic community depends on a strong information system and engaged citizens who take advantage of that information.[1] The Commission maintained there are three dimensions of the system: a robust, diverse supply of information, a sophisticated communications infrastructure for delivering information, and residents with the skills needed to access that information and use it in effective ways to address their community's needs. Further, Commission members said they believed there were several key indicators of information systems that performed well:

1) Quality journalism through local newspapers, local television and radio stations, and online sources
2) A local government with a committed policy on transparency
3) Citizens with effective opportunities to have their voices heard and to affect public policy
4) Ready access to information that enhances quality of life, including information provided by trusted intermediary organizations in the community on a variety of subjects
5) High speed internet available to all citizens
6) Local schools with computer and high-speed internet access, as well as curricula that support digital and media literacy
7) A vibrant public library, or other public center for information that provides digital resources and professional assistance
8) A majority of government information and services online, accessible through a central and easy to use portal

The aim of the Monitor Institute-Pew Internet work was to try to examine these different components of the information systems in three communities. The Monitor Institute was also asked to create an easy-to-use set of tools to help community leaders assess and improve their local information ecology. Version 1.0 of the **Community Information Toolkit** can be accessed at www.infotoolkit.org. In addition, there was an opportunity to probe more deeply with the data that was collected in the pilot sites, especially those from telephone surveys of 500 residents in each community. Those findings make up the core of this report. They sometimes highlight consistent patterns of adoption, impact, and interaction among the features of local information systems. At the same time, there are varying results depending on the community. Here are some of the key findings:

In their activities and attitudes, people show how the information system parts fit together. But some elements are difficult to assess independently: Community residents showed in their answers how they feel the system works and how the different elements of the system are connected. There were notable associations between some of the indicators and civic outcomes. For example: Those who are avid news consumers are more likely than others to be civically active. Broadband users and library patrons are more likely than others to feel good about their ability to gather information to meet their needs. Those who have found helpful government information online feel better than others about their own ability to make their communities better. Those who think their children are getting good computer- and information-evaluation training at school feel better than others about the overall performance of the schools and several other local institutions. More generally, there were correlations between citizens' sense of how the information system as a whole was performing and their overall satisfaction with their

---

[1] See the full commission report at: http://www.knightcomm.org/

community, their evaluation of existing stocks of information, and their belief in their own capacity to drive community change. Yet several of the indicators are difficult to measure and assess independently without complicated and expensive methodologies – notably, the quality of a community's journalism, the effectiveness of technology programs at schools, the availability of "quality of life" information from community organizations, and the "effective opportunities" for citizens to have their voices heard.

Yet several of the indicators are difficult to measure and assess independently without complicated and expensive methodologies – notably, the quality of a community's journalism, the effectiveness of technology programs at schools, the availability of "quality of life" information from community organizations, and "effective opportunities" for citizens to have their voices heard. Moreover, many of the local leaders who attended community workshops for this research initiative argued there was another variable that mattered in understanding the effectiveness of local information systems. That variable related to the flow of information – to citizens' capacities to search for, aggregate, process, and act on information that is relevant to their needs. The community leaders reported that it was often the case that their stakeholders were not aware of the most useful information in the community and not certain how to act effectively on the information they did have. They also noted there were times when local governments were not effectively communicating to residents what information was available.

Those who think local government does well in sharing information are also more likely to be satisfied with other parts of civic life: Residents who said in the surveys that their local government was good at sharing information were more likely to feel satisfied with a host of other aspects of civic life. Citizens who believed that their government was forthcoming about its activities were more likely than others to feel better about these things: the overall quality of their community; the ability of the entire information environment of their community to give them the information that matters; the overall performance of their local government; and the performance of all manner of civic and journalistic institutions ranging from the fire department to the libraries to local newspaper and TV stations.

In addition, government transparency is associated with residents' feelings of efficacy and empowerment: Those who think their government shares information well are more likely to say that people like them can have an impact on government. It might be the case that signals from government that "we want to be open about what we do" make people think they can take advantage of that openness and influence the way the government operates.

This is not to say that people in these three communities feel their local governments are great at sharing information. Indeed, their judgments about government transparency were not uniformly high. Residents of San Jose were the most likely to say their government did "very well" in sharing information about its dealings and operations: 20% said their local government shared information "very well" and another 52% said their local government did "pretty well" with disclosing information. This contrasted with the residents of Philadelphia who gave their city significantly poorer grades – 12% said "very well" and 43% said "pretty well." Macon residents were in the middle – 15% at "very well" and 49% at "pretty well."

Those who are happy about their local government's transparency also feel good about the performance of other local institutions

% of residents in Philadelphia, San Jose, Macon who rate local institutions as doing a good or excellent job

	Those who say local gov does very/pretty well sharing info N=953	Those who say local gov does not very/not too well sharing info N=457
Quite satisfied with their community*	65%	45%
Feel people like me can have a big/moderate impact on the community	72%	59%
Feel news and info sources give them all the information that matters	30%	11%
Fire dept doing good/excellent job	90%	79%
Libraries doing good/excellent job	82%	64%
Local TV stations doing good/excellent job	79%	63%
Local newspapers doing good/excellent job	76%	44%
Police dept doing good/excellent job	72%	46%
Local cultural organizations doing good/excellent job	57%	32%
Public schools doing good/excellent job	55%	32%
Local business organizations doing good/excellent job	55%	31%
City government doing good/excellent job	38%	12%

*Residents were asked to rate their satisfaction on a 1-5 scale with 5 being "extremely satisfied." These were the respondents who rated their community either a 4 or a 5

Source: Monitor Institute - Pew Research Center's Internet & American Life Project November 2010 surveys in Philadelphia, San Jose, and Macon. N=1,510 adults age 18 and older in the three communities combined, including 398 reached via cell phone. Interviews conducted in English and Spanish.

Despite the business troubles in the news industry, residents are pleased with the performance of local news organizations and feel they generally present diverse perspectives on community news. Many think they are getting more local information than they did five years ago. If they felt they were getting more material now, they were also more likely to be civically engaged: The news ecosystem in many communities, including in these three, has been in severe financial difficulty in recent years. Yet people in these towns rate local news operations quite favorably and those good opinions are very similar to the judgments residents offered in surveys commissioned by the Knight Foundation in 2002 before journalism's business problems were acute.

- 74% say local TV stations are doing an excellent or good job
- 69% say local radio stations are doing an excellent or good job
- 68% say the local newspaper is doing an excellent or good job

- 53% say local specialized publications such as magazines, local business journals, or non-profit newsletters are doing an excellent or good job
- 50% say internet sites that focus on local affairs are doing an excellent or good job.

Additionally, more than two-thirds of the respondents said the four main news platforms -- television, newspapers, internet, and radio – presented diverse perspectives in their communities.

In spite of the dramatic staffing cutbacks at traditional news organizations and the economic stresses in newsrooms, only about a tenth of the people in these towns say they are getting less information about their communities than they got five years ago, while substantially more residents say they are getting more information (53% say that in San Jose; 44% in Philadelphia; 36% say that in Macon.) The rise of the internet as a local information source is a potential factor driving people's sense that more local information is available to them. For instance, the internet is cited by citizens as one of the leading sources of information when they are seeking information about local jobs, topics that are of special personal interest. Still, while local residents sensed that they are receiving in aggregate more local information than before, we did not probe more specifically whether these perceptions hold true for specific areas of reporting and news coverage that other studies have suggested have been affected by disruptions in the journalism industry, such as local education coverage, government affairs coverage, and arts coverage.

Those who said they were getting more local news and information were more likely than others to report they are very satisfied with the community, participate in some civic activities such as attending meetings and signing petitions, feel like people like them can have a big impact on the community, salute the performance of local institutions, and use the internet to gather information about local government.

Citizen interest in news has long been found to be associated with civic engagement. That holds true in these communities. If people are news junkies who regularly use multiple news sources such as the newspaper, TV stations, and the internet, they are more likely to be civically active in several ways, including: attending meetings, working with fellow citizens to solve community problems, and interacting with news organizations. Of course, the relationship likely goes in the other direction, too. The civically engaged will naturally seek out more information because they will need the information to pursue whatever they are pursuing.

Broadband users are sometimes *less* satisfied than others with community life. That raises the possibility that upgrades in a local information system might produce more critical, activist citizens: Perhaps the most surprising finding in the surveys was that in some circumstances, broadband users are more likely to be critical of elements of their local information ecosystem and less likely to feel that the local information system could produce information they might need. In these communities, San Jose distances itself from the other communities in online connectivity, with 85% of its adults using the internet and 76% of San Jose residents having a broadband connection at home. That compares with 66% of adults in Philadelphia who use the internet and 57% who have broadband connections at home; and 64% in Macon who use the internet and 50% who have broadband at home. The most recent data from the Pew Internet Project is that 79% of American adults use the internet and 67% of all Americans have broadband connections at home.

It is not clear in these surveys why broadband connections are correlated with lower perceptions of community life and local information systems. Perhaps, as some people take advantage of broadband connections they become exposed to more critical information about local government and organizations and they become more aware of information and conversations about community problems. Perhaps, too, broadband users' expectations are higher about the availability of information and the ease of finding it – so, they would give lower performance grades if the local information system did not meet those higher expectations. Whatever the reason, having a home broadband connection was _**negatively**_ correlated at the 95% level in at least one of the cities with users' views that:

- Their local government is doing a good job – in San Jose and Philadelphia
- The news sources in their community deliver all the information they need – in Philadelphia
- Local schools are doing a good job – in Philadelphia
- Local non-profit organizations do a good job helping the poor – in Philadelphia
- They are very confident they could find local information to help them understand how local politicians are performing – in Philadelphia
- They are very confident they could find local information for finding a job – in San Jose
- They are very confident they could find local information in an emergency – in San Jose

At the same time, broadband connectivity does seem to have a clear civic payoff in at least one way for communities: Those with home broadband are significantly more likely to use the internet for civic activities, such as using email and social media to talk about local issues.

Residents in these towns also offered mixed views about the personal benefits they get from high-speed connections. We asked internet users in each community to assess the impact that internet connectivity had on several dimensions of their lives and the pattern was that internet use for personal matters had a greater impact on users than internet use for community-related matters:

- 69% of the internet users in the three communities said that internet had made a major impact on their ability to learn new things.
- 48% of the internet users in the three communities said that internet had made a major impact on their ability to manage their health or the health of other members of their family.
- 34% of the internet users in the three communities said that internet had made a major impact on their ability to participate in their community.
- 24% of the internet users in the three communities said that internet had made a major impact on their ability to interact with government officials and politicians.

Finally, a majority residents in the three communities agreed with the Knight Commission that having easy access to broadband was very important or pretty important: 78% of those in San Jose believe that; 67% of those in Macon believe that; and 63% of Philadelphians believe that. Interestingly, the people who already have broadband are much more likely than others to say access to it is important. Non-broadband users do not feel the same urgency to access as those who already have it.

Social media like Facebook and Twitter are emerging as key parts of the civic landscape and mobile connectivity is beginning to affect people's interactions with civic life: In these communities, residents are beginning to use social media to learn about their community and share information about what they observe and know. They also use email to stay in touch with community matters. Cell phones, for some, are becoming gateways to local news:

- In the three communities combined, 32% of the internet users <u>get local news from social networking sites</u> like Facebook, MySpace or LinkedIn.
- In the three locales, 19% of the internet users <u>get local news from blogs</u> that focus on local subjects.
- In the three locales, 19% of the internet users <u>get local news from an email listserv or group email</u> list that focuses on local matters.
- In the three locales, 12% of the internet users <u>use their cell phones to get local news either from websites or alerts</u> that are sent to their phones.
- In the three locales, 7% of the internet users <u>get local news from Twitter.</u>

On the participatory side:

- In the three locales, 32% of the internet users have <u>posted updates and local news on a social networking site like Facebook or MySpace.</u>
- In the three communities combined, 17% of internet users have <u>commented on issues on a local news website.</u>
- In the three communities combined, 14% of internet users <u>discussed local issues and news on email listservs.</u>
- In the three communities combined, 12% of internet users had <u>written on blogs</u> about local subjects.
- In the three communities combined, 6% of the internet users had <u>posted material on Twitter.</u>

People use different sources for different types of local information: The news and information ecosystem is fracturing. When it comes to the most important sources of information for people on particular subjects, there is considerable variance among the communities and among the topics about which people were questioned. In broad strokes, newspapers and television were deemed the most important sources for general information about the communities and residents' neighborhoods, and the internet was the third most important source. But when it came to personally-relevant information such as looking for jobs or finding material about topics that were especially important, the internet shot to the top of the list of sources.

There was notable variance among the communities when residents were asked about the best source of information for several key subjects

% of residents in Philadelphia, San Jose, Macon who identified each source as most important.

What is the most important source of information about ...	Philadelphia N=503	Macon N=503	San Jose N=504
Your city			
Printed newspapers /magazine	30%	37%	30%
Television	33%	33%	23%
Radio	7%	4%	5%
Online	21%	15%	29%
Community newsletter	2%	2%	4%
Other people (word of mouth)	3%	3%	4%
Your neighborhood			
Printed newspapers /magazine	33%	27%	37%
Television	19%	25%	14%
Radio	2%	4%	3%
Online	11%	11%	15%
Community newsletter	13%	10%	15%
Other people (word of mouth)	12%	10%	10%
Job-related information			
Printed newspapers /magazine	28%	24%	26%
Television	9%	16%	5%
Radio	2%	1%	2%
Online	40%	35%	51%
Community newsletter	1%	0%	0%
Other people (word of mouth)	3%	3%	4%
Topics that are of special interest to you personally			
Printed newspapers /magazine	25%	25%	24%
Television	23%	27%	16%
Radio	5%	6%	4%
Online	35%	29%	45%
Community newsletter	3%	1%	1%
Other people (word of mouth)	3%	3%	4%

Source: Monitor Institute - Pew Research Center's Internet & American Life Project November 2010 surveys in Philadelphia, San Jose, and Macon. N=1,510 adults age 18 and older in the three communities combined, including 398 reached via cell phone. Interviews conducted in English and Spanish.

If citizens feel empowered, communities get benefits in both directions. Those who believe they can impact their community are more likely to be engaged in civic activities and are more likely to be satisfied with their towns: We asked citizens to assess how much impact they believe people like them can have in making their communities better places to live. Roughly a third of residents in each of the communities said they and others like them could have a major impact. Those who believed that were more likely than others to participate in civic activities online and offline and more likely to feel that the local information ecosystem could serve their needs. Those who felt people like them could have a major impact were:

- More likely to be satisfied with their community overall – in Philadelphia
- More likely to be civically active in offline ways such as attending meetings, working with others on local problems, contacting local news media – in Macon and San Jose
- More likely to say the local government was doing a good job – in Philadelphia and San Jose
- More likely to say they are confident they could get information from local sources that would tell them if local politicians were doing a good job – in Philadelphia and San Jose
- More likely to say local cultural organizations are doing a good job – in all three communities
- More likely to say local schools were doing a good job – in Philadelphia and San Jose
- More likely to say they are confident they could get information from local sources that would help them improve their skills and knowledge to get a better job – in Philadelphia and San Jose

Leaders in each community who participated in workshops related to the research expressed differing perspectives on whether their communities provided effective opportunities for citizens to have their voices heard. In Macon there were leaders of several traditional groups with national charters such as the Lions Club and Junior League. Many of the local leaders expressed frustration, saying that many local civic groups served only one portion of the community and that the government was not active enough in providing opportunities to discuss community-wide matters. In San Jose and Philadelphia, on the other hand, there was a somewhat more diverse mixture of groups. Local leaders in these communities said they thought there were sufficient opportunities to share their opinions, with each other and with the government. Still, they also expressed concern that these opportunities came only in segregated geographic or demographic communities. In these workshops, local leaders said they wanted to create opportunities for citizens to collaborate across geographic and topical boundaries and collectively develop and share their opinions about local issues.

Unfamiliarity does not necessarily breed discontent. Many citizens give their local information systems a vote of confidence even if they do not have direct contact with or knowledge of some of the system's features. For a notable number of people, contentment with the local media ecology is not necessarily born of patronage or need. They express satisfaction with the quality of the environment even if they do not necessarily have any current personal information need that they want to address or even if they have not recently interacted with parts of the system. It might be the case that people's general good feelings come from what they have learned second hand. Examples:

- 57% of these residents say they have been to the local library in the past 12 months, yet fully 83% of residents (including many non-patrons) say they think the local library has the resources they might need to do research that is important to them. An even greater proportion of residents – 88% – say they think the local library has the necessary computers and internet connections they might require if an information-hunt were necessary.
- 34% of residents say they have had interactions with emergency personnel or police or fire fighters in the past 12 months, yet 86% say the fire department is doing an excellent or good job and 64% say the police department is doing an excellent or good job.
- 40% of residents have had interactions with teachers or administrators at local schools and 34% of the residents say they have attended a meeting on local or school affairs, yet 47% say they think the local schools are doing an excellent or good job and fully 76% say they believe the schools have classes or programs to teach students about how to get good, accurate information.

Local community residents employ a range of strategies to find civic information: the three most common approaches are to use Google, to search local websites, and to tap their informal networks. In each of the communities, some residents participated in a "scavenger hunt" for local civic information. They were asked to show their search strategies for such things as: accessing local government services and discovering the budget for local schools. Participants in all three communities commonly used Google to search and find this information. They also frequently used the websites of the prominent local news organizations, such as the city newspaper or television station. The consistency with which these researchers targeted local internet sources in each community was interesting, and suggests a collective understanding of the best online sources. For example, in Philadelphia most of the residents that participated used Philly.com (the website of the Philadelphia Inquirer), and in Macon they used 13maz.com (local television station) and Macon.com (website for the Macon Telegraph). Finally, in each community the participants resorted at times to querying informal networks when they knew someone who worked in a relevant position. For example, many participants contacted someone they knew who worked in the school administration to find the budget for schools in their area.

Each of these communities has a web portal for government and civic information, yet only a little more than a third of their residents were fully aware of that. Moreover, in the opinion surveys, we found that many who tried to use the internet to get local civic information could not always find what they were seeking. Only a quarter of these residents said that when they did searches for local civic information they always found what they were seeking. Yet even when they found what they were seeking, only 37% said the information presented to them was very clear and easy to understand.

Perhaps as a result, one strong yearning residents expressed was for a central location for civic information that is maintained by the government. More than three-quarters of the respondents in these three communities (78%) said it was "very important" that a government website be set up for this and another 17% said it was "somewhat important."

The information people seek online about their communities. Cell phones are becoming a key tool to access important material.

% of internet users in Philadelphia, Macon, San Jose who seek various kinds of local information online

	Philadelphia n=342	Macon n=348	San Jose n=433
Transportation services or local road conditions	54%	24%	50%
How they got the info online			
Cell phone	8%	7%	7%
Computer	65%	67%	62%
Both	27%	26%	31%
Activities of your local government	39%	30%	37%
How they got the info online			
Cell phone	2%	0%	1%
Computer	78%	89%	80%
Both	20%	11%	20%
Your local schools	35%	42%	44%
How they got the info online			
Cell phone	6%	6%	2%
Computer	66%	80%	76%
Both	28%	14%	22%
Materials that might be available at local libraries	35%	33%	48%
How they got the info online			
Cell phone	5%	1%	2%
Computer	65%	78%	80%
Both	30%	20%	17%
Property taxes	30%	39%	29%
How they got the info online			
Cell phone	2%	2%	1%
Computer	86%	91%	88%
Both	13%	7%	11%
Safety services such as police and fire protection	18%	18%	21%
How they got the info online			
Cell phone	11%	4%	4%
Computer	68%	74%	76%
Both	21%	21%	20%
% who always find the material they were seeking	25%	25%	28%
% of those who found the information who say information is very clear/easy to understand	37%	37%	38%

Source: Monitor Institute - Pew Research Center's Internet & American Life Project November 2010 surveys in Philadelphia, San Jose, and Macon. N=1,510 adults age 18 and older in the three communities combined, including 398 reached via cell phone. Interviews conducted in English and Spanish.

San Jose stands apart: As communities try to understand what thriving information systems look like and what kinds of benefits they produce, our first examination of these communities shows that San Jose might provide particularly interesting evidence. The town stands apart in several ways among the three communities. San Jose residents expressed the highest level of overall satisfaction with their town. They are the most wired. They are the most likely to connect to the internet by cell phone. They are the most praising of their local institutions, including fire, police, schools, city government, libraries, local cultural organizations, and local nonprofits that help the poor. Further, they are more content with their government's willingness to share information. They give higher grades to the local newspaper. They are heavier patrons of libraries. They are more aware of the local government's web operations. They are more likely to say that the internet is a preferred source of information on local topics and more likely to say the internet presents a diverse range of points of view. And they are more likely to say they are getting more information now compared with five years ago.

Some of these differences are likely to be rooted in economic and socio-economic differences among the communities. The San Jose survey sample showed that compared with the other two communities people in San Jose had higher household incomes, were more likely to have full-time jobs, and more likely to have college or graduate degrees. Some of the advantages residents feel about their information system could stem from that relative affluence and the economic vitality in the community.

Still, there are suggestions in these findings that a more robust information system brings its own rewards in citizen satisfaction and the performance of the organs of civic culture. These findings are not so clear or strong that they can end discussions about what elements of the information ecosystem are most critical or how the parts of the system work with each other. More findings in other communities, perhaps employing other methodologies, could help bring these important issues more clearly into focus.

This research and the input Monitor got in workshops with leaders in each of the cities could be taken as heartening news by other communities that want to explore their own information ecology and the way citizens operate in it. We did not establish causality here – for instance, that greater government transparency provides benefits to a host of civic organizations or that broadband-adoption initiatives will heighten citizens' critical thinking about their community or that higher-quality journalism will encourage more people to turn out for town meetings. Yet these possibilities emerge in the answers citizens and their leaders gave. We learned that conversations about a locality's information needs can bring striking vitality to the ways people think about how to make their community's better.